THE ILLUSTRATED DICTIONARY OF

MACHINES

D0728250

Reader's notes

The entries in this dictionary have several features to help you understand more about the word you are looking up.

- Each entry is introduced by its headword. All the headwords in the dictionary are arranged in alphabetical order.

- Each headword is followed by a part of speech to show whether the word is used as a noun, adjective, verb or prefix.

- Each entry begins with a sentence that uses the headword as its subject.

- Words that are bold in an entry are cross references. You can look them up in this dictionary to find out more information about the topic.

- The sentence in italics at the end of an entry helps you to see how the headword can be used.

- Many of the entries are illustrated. The labels on the illustrations highlight all the key points of information.

- Many of the labels on the illustrations have their own entries in the dictionary and can therefore be used as cross references.

THE ILLUSTRATED DICTIONARY OF

MACHINES

Contributors
Michael Pollard
Merilyn Holme

CLAREMONT
BOOKS

Copyright © 1995 Godfrey Cave Associates
First published 1995 in this format by
Claremont Books
42 Bloomsbury Street
London WC1B 3QJ

Series editor: Merilyn Holme
Assistant editor: Maureen Bailey

Design: Steven Hulbert
Illustrations: Peter Bull; Jeremy Gower and Matthew White (B.L.
Kearley Ltd); Simon Tegg

Consultant: Malcolm Tucker, Engineering Consultant, Bath, U.K.

All rights reserved.
No part of this publication may be reproduced,
stored in a retrieval system, or transmitted, in any form or by any means,
electronic, mechanical, photocopying, recording or otherwise
without the prior permission of the copyright holder.

Printed in Great Britain.

ISBN 1 85471 651 4

A

accelerate   *verb*
Accelerate means to increase in speed. An object accelerates when a **force** makes it move faster.
The car accelerated round the last bend and won the race.
acceleration   *noun*

accelerator   *noun*
1. An accelerator is a pedal or **lever** which releases the power of an **engine** and makes it run faster. It controls the flow of fuel to the engine.
The driver put his foot on the accelerator and caught up with the car in front.
2. An accelerator is a machine which greatly increases the speed of particles of matter by giving them an electric charge.
Accelerators are used in medicine and industry.

accelerometer   *noun*
An accelerometer is a device that measures the rate at which a machine's speed increases. It shows the measurement on a dial.
The jet plane's accelerometer showed how fast its speed increased as it dived towards the ground.

aerial   *adjective*
Aerial is a word which describes an object that travels through the air, such as an **aeroplane**. It also describes something that is carried out in the air, such as aerial photography.
The aircraft carried out an aerial survey of the coastline.

aerial   *noun*
An aerial is a long piece of wire, a rod or a dish. It transmits or receives radio signals. An aerial is connected to a **transmitter** or a **receiver**.
A radio receives signals through its aerial and changes them into sounds.

aerofoil   *noun*
An aerofoil is a curved surface which is held up, or supported, by the flow of air around it. Aerofoils help **aircraft** to stay in the air and to change direction.
Air flows more quickly over the top of an aerofoil than underneath it.

aeroplane   *noun*
An aeroplane is an **aircraft** with one or more pairs of wings. Fighters, bombers and **airliners** are all aeroplanes.
We flew by aeroplane when we went on holiday.

aerosol   *noun*
An aerosol is a fine mist of liquid or powder. The mist is sprayed out of a can by pressing a button. This kind of can is often called an aerosol.
She used an aerosol to kill the flies in the kitchen.

after-burner   *noun*
An after-burner is a machine that sprays fuel into the exhaust pipe of a **jet engine**. This gives the engine extra power.
The fighter pilot used his after-burners to put on more speed.

after-burner

aileron *noun*

An aileron is a hinged flap on the rear, or trailing, edge of each wing of an **aeroplane**. It is placed near the tip of the wing. Ailerons make the plane roll from side to side. The movements of an aileron are controlled by the pilot.
Moving the ailerons helps the aeroplane to turn to the left or right.

air cleaner *noun*

An air cleaner is a machine used in industry. It removes harmful chemicals and dust from gases produced by factories and **power stations**.
Air cleaners help to prevent pollution of the atmosphere.

air conditioner *noun*

An air conditioner is a machine that controls the state of the air in a building. It pumps stale, hot air away and replaces it with clean, cool air. Air conditioners can also be used in motor vehicles.
The office was fresh and cool in summer because it had an air conditioner.

air hammer *noun*

An air hammer is a **pneumatic machine**. It uses **compressed air** to push the hammer head down.
The factory was noisy with the sound of air hammers.

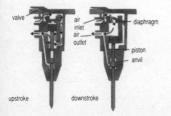

valve · air inlet · air outlet · diaphragm · piston · anvil · upstroke · downstroke

air ionizer *noun*

An air ionizer is a machine which removes electrons from negatively-charged atoms in the air to make them positively-charged. Atoms carrying an electric charge, either positive or negative, are called ions. An air ionizer is used in a room where there is a lot of electrical equipment. It helps to prevent the room from feeling stuffy.
An air ionizer was installed in the computer room.

aircraft ► page 8

airliner *noun*

An airliner is an **aeroplane** designed to carry passengers or goods. Airliners fly on regular routes between one airport and another. Usually airliners can travel great distances without the need to refuel.
The Concorde is a supersonic airliner that flies between London and New York at speeds faster than sound.

airport crash tender *noun*

An airport crash tender is a vehicle that is on duty whenever **aircraft** take off or land at an airport. It has fire-fighting and other equipment for use in an emergency.
The aeroplane landed on one engine and the airport crash tender rushed to the scene.

airship *noun*

An airship is an **aircraft**. Its cabin and engine are slung beneath a huge balloon filled with a light gas called helium. The balloon is stretched over an **aluminium** frame. An airship can fly because the gas inside it is lighter, or less dense, than air.
Airships use tall towers called mooring towers to take off and land.

airspeed indicator *noun*

An airspeed indicator is an instrument on the **control panel** of an **aircraft**. It shows how fast the aircraft is travelling through the air.
The pilot checked the airspeed indicator to see if the aircraft would arrive on time.

alarm system   *noun*
An alarm system is a device that gives warning of dangers such as smoke, fire or intruders. Alarm systems use electronic **sensors** to keep a constant check for danger.
The alarm system was set off by someone climbing over the factory wall.

alcohol breath tester   *noun*
An alcohol breath tester is a small device that is used by police to check whether a driver has been drinking too much alcohol. The driver breathes into a tube, and the tester shows how much alcohol is in the driver's blood.
The alcohol breath tester showed that she was unfit to drive.

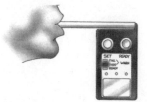

alloy   *noun*
An alloy is a mixture of metals or other materials. It is made by melting two or more kinds of material together. Alloys are often stronger than the materials they are made from, and stand up to heat better.
Alloys are used for many parts of jet engines.

alternating current   *noun*
Alternating current is a flow of **electricity** that behaves in a special way. It grows stronger and then weaker and then changes direction. This takes place many times every second.
The electricity supply in most homes is alternating current.

alternator   *noun*
An alternator is a machine which produces, or generates, **alternating current**. The shaft of the alternator is made to spin at great speed and is surrounded by a magnet.
Most power stations contain alternators which are driven by steam turbines.

altimeter   *noun*
An altimeter is an instrument on the **control panel** of an **aircraft**. It shows how high the aircraft is flying. An altimeter measures the weight of the air pressing around the aircraft, at ground level and at height. This weight of air is called the atmospheric pressure.
The pilot looked at the altimeter to see if he had reached his planned height.

aluminium   *noun*
Aluminium is a soft, silvery metal which is very light in weight. It is taken out, or extracted, from an ore called bauxite, when the bauxite is heated.
Aluminium is used for making an aircraft's fuselage and wings.

amplifier   *noun*
An amplifier is a device that changes a weak **electric signal** into a stronger one. It also cuts out unwanted sounds that sometimes come from disturbance in the atmosphere. Most amplifiers use transistors linked by **electric circuits**.
Radios and record-players contain amplifiers.
amplify   *verb*

aircraft   *noun*
An aircraft is any kind of machine that travels by air. It may have wings like an **aeroplane** or rotor blades like a **helicopter**, or it may be an **airship**.
We saw many different kinds of aircraft at the airport.

A large passenger aeroplane has four powerful jet engines. It can carry more than 500 passengers at a speed of 965 kilometres per hour. The aeroplane can travel more than 11,000 kilometres without having to take on more fuel.

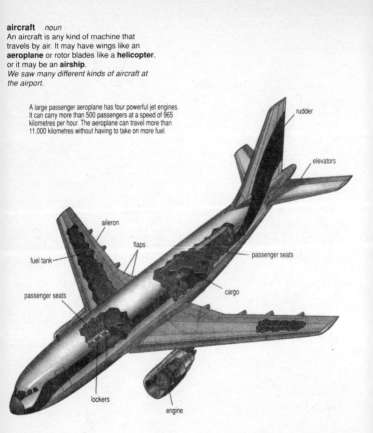

rudder

elevators

aileron

flaps

passenger seats

fuel tank

passenger seats

cargo

lockers

engine

A helicopter is powered by two spinning blades called rotors.

A hang glider is held in the air by wind currents.

A glider looks like an aeroplane, but it is powered by the wind instead of an engine.

An airship has a large balloon, or envelope, filled with helium gas and shaped like an aerofoil.

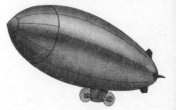

How an aeroplane flies

An aeroplane wing is shaped like an aerofoil. As the air pushes over the curved, upper surface of the wing, its pressure drops. The air under the wing moves more slowly, so its pressure stays higher. It pushes the aeroplane up into the air and holds it there.

An aeroplane needs powerful engines to give it enough thrust to overcome its weight and the drag of the fuselage and wings.

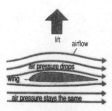

lift

airflow

air pressure drops

wing

air pressure stays the same

direction of flight

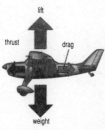

lift

thrust

drag

weight

analogue *adjective*

Analogue describes something that is like, or similar to, something else. It is used for machines that copy the way things are in real life. A **watch** with a dial and hands is an analogue watch. Its hands copy the movement of the Earth round the Sun. A watch which shows only numerals is called a **digital** watch.

The minute hand of an analogue clock takes one hour to move round the dial.

anchor escapement *noun*

An anchor escapement is part of a clockwork **watch** or **clock**. It rocks to and fro and controls the unwinding of the spring. This makes the hands of the clock tick forward. There is a tooth on each arm of the anchor escapement which connects with a **cog wheel**.

The anchor escapement gets its name from its shape, which is like a ship's anchor.

anemometer *noun*

An anemometer is an instrument for measuring the speed of the wind. The most common type of anemometer is made up of three or four cups mounted on a pole. An anemometer is placed in an open space. The wind drives the cups round, and a counter mechanism in the instrument records how fast the cups spin. The wind speed is then shown on a display panel.

The anemometer showed that the wind was blowing a full gale.

aneroid barometer *noun*

An aneroid barometer is an instrument for measuring atmospheric pressure. It has a thin, round, metal box that contains a partial **vacuum**. The pressure of the air outside makes the sides of the box move in or out. A needle shows this movement on a dial.

The aneroid barometer showed that the atmospheric pressure was high, so it would be a fine day.

antenna *noun*

Antenna is another name for an **aerial**.

The receiver's antenna picked up the radio signals.

anvil *noun*

An anvil is a block of **iron** or **steel** that is used to shape metal objects. One end is shaped like an oblong block, the other like a cone.

The blacksmith hammered the horseshoe on the anvil.

aperture *noun*

An aperture is a hole or an opening. The **lens** of a **camera** has an aperture through which light passes. The light entering the aperture makes an image on the film inside the camera.

In most cameras, the size of the aperture can be changed to let different amounts of light through.

appliance ► page 12

aqualung *noun*

An aqualung is a piece of equipment used by an underwater diver. It is made up of metal tanks of **compressed air**. The diver breathes air from the tanks through a tube and **valve**.

The diver adjusted the mouthpiece of his aqualung so that he could breathe more easily.

Archimedes' screw *noun*

Archimedes' screw is a method of raising water from one level to another. A screw-shaped channel turns inside a hollow shaft and carries the water upwards. Archimedes was a Greek scientist who lived more than 2,200 years ago.

Archimedes' screw is still used in some places to water fields where crops are grown.

asbestos *noun*

Asbestos is a mineral. It can be separated into fibres and then woven into sheets. It can also be mixed with materials such as rubber or cement. Asbestos does not burn and can be used to protect people and objects against heat. Breathing asbestos dust is very harmful, and for this reason asbestos is being used less and less.

Fire-fighters often wear asbestos suits to protect them from the heat of a fire.

asphalt *noun*

Asphalt is a mixture of a black, tarry substance called bitumen, and sand. It melts when heated. Asphalt is used to make road surfaces.

The road workers gave the road a new covering of asphalt.

assembly line ▶ page 14

auto- *prefix*

Auto- is a prefix that describes a machine which affects or controls itself.

An automatic machine does not need a person to control it.

autocue *noun*

An autocue is a kind of **electronic** device that is used by television presenters. It projects an image of the presenter's script onto a sheet of glass in front of the camera lens. As the presenter reads the script, the autocue shows the next few words or sentences.

A television newscaster does not need to learn the script because it can be read from the autocue.

automatic governor *noun*

An automatic governor is a **device** which controls the speed of a machine. It controls the amount of fuel used by the machine. If the machine starts to run too fast, the automatic governor slows it down to the correct speed.

The automatic governor kept the machine running at an even speed.

automatic machine *noun*

An automatic machine is a machine that works without human help.

A slot machine which sells drinks or chocolate is an automatic machine.

automation *noun*

Automation is a word which describes how work in some factories is done entirely by **machines**. **Computers** usually control the machines.

There are only a few workers in this factory because automation does most of the work.

11

appliance *noun*

An appliance is a machine used for a special purpose. **Washing machines** and **food processors** are examples of appliances.
A vacuum cleaner is an appliance that most people have in their homes.

A grinding wheel polishes and sharpens a metal surface.

A lathe is an industrial appliance that shaves small pieces off a rotating section of metal.

A saw cuts metal to a certain size.

A drill makes holes in a strip, sheet or block of metal.

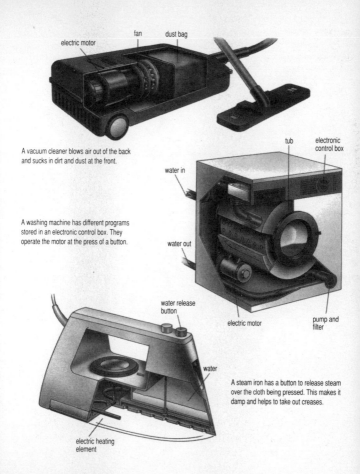

electric motor · fan · dust bag

A vacuum cleaner blows air out of the back and sucks in dirt and dust at the front.

A washing machine has different programs stored in an electronic control box. They operate the motor at the press of a button.

water in · tub · electronic control box · water out · electric motor · pump and filter

water release button · water · electric heating element

A steam iron has a button to release steam over the cloth being pressed. This makes it damp and helps to take out creases.

assembly line *noun*

An assembly line is a row of machines found in many factories. Each machine carries out a different stage in the manufacturing process. Many machines in an assembly line are worked by **computers** or **robots**. **Products** as small as a personal stereo or as large as a tractor are produced on an assembly line.

Cars are built on an assembly line.

A sheet of steel is made ready for shaping into the body of a car.

The finished car

14

All the sections of the car body have been cut, pressed into shape and put together, or assembled. The body is dipped in a fluid to protect it against rust. Then it is given a coat of primer paint.

The car body is sprayed with paint. Then parts such as the wheels, windscreens and fuse box are fitted.

The engine is tested carefully before it is fitted into the car. All the inside parts, such as the seats and carpets, are also put in at this stage.

The windows, bumpers and wheels are covered before the car is given its final painting.

15

automobile   *noun*
An automobile is a road **vehicle**. It is powered by an **internal combustion engine**. Most automobiles burn **petrol** in their engines, but some use **diesel fuel**.
The family went on holiday in their automobile.

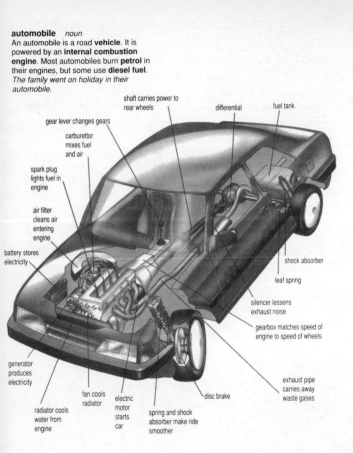

shaft carries power to rear wheels

differential

fuel tank

gear lever changes gears

carburettor mixes fuel and air

spark plug lights fuel in engine

air filter cleans air entering engine

battery stores electricity

shock absorber

leaf spring

silencer lessens exhaust noise

gearbox matches speed of engine to speed of wheels

generator produces electricity

fan cools radiator

electric motor starts car

disc brake

exhaust pipe carries away waste gases

radiator cools water from engine

spring and shock absorber make ride smoother

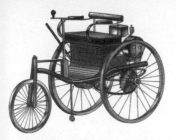

Karl Benz's Patent Motor Car, 1886, had a top speed of less than 16 kilometres per hour.

The Ford Model T, 1915, was built on an assembly line in the United States of America.

The Bugatti Royale, 1927, was the longest car ever made. It had a 12.7 litre engine and a top speed of 193 kilometres per hour.

The Jaguar XK120 of 1948 was the first of a new kind of streamlined sports car. Its engine design is still used today.

The German Volkswagen Beetle was first made in 1945. It is one of the most popular cars of all time.

A car of the future will have a sleek, streamlined body and may run on electricity or solar power.

automobile ► page 16

autopilot   *noun*
An autopilot is a machine on the flight deck
of an **aeroplane**. It **automatically** controls
the direction in which the aeroplane flies. It
has **gyroscopic sensors** which control the
aircraft's movements.
*The captain of the airliner set the autopilot to
fly the aeroplane due south.*

axle   *noun*
An axle is a rod. It fits into the centre of a
wheel so that the wheel can turn, or revolve,
round it.
*A wheelbarrow has one wheel on a very
short axle.*

B

baggage scanner   *noun*
A baggage scanner is a machine which
allows people to see what is inside a closed
suitcase or bag. X-rays make the luggage
appear transparent on a television screen.
Baggage scanners are used at airports and
at other security centres.
*The baggage scanner showed that there
was a gun inside the suitcase.*

balance   *noun*
A balance is a kind of **weighing machine**. It
is used for making accurate measurements
of weight. Some balances work by stretching
a spring. Others have a beam, balanced in
the centre. The object to be weighed is
attached to one end and a known weight,
such as a kilogram, is attached to the other.
*The scientist used a balance to find the
weight of one grain of sand.*

baler   *noun*
A baler is a machine which makes bundles
out of materials such as straw or waste
paper. It ties the bundles so that they can be
moved easily.
*After the wheat had been harvested, a baler
made the straw into round bales.*

ball race   *noun*
A ball race is a part of some machines. It is
made from two steel rings which fit one
inside the other. The rings are kept apart by
steel balls called ball bearings. When the
two rings move, the ball bearings also move
and make the movement smooth.
*Bicycles have ball races in the hubs of their
wheels.*

ballcock   *noun*
A ballcock is a device which controls the flow of liquids. It floats on the surface of the liquid. When the container is nearly full, a **valve** attached to the ballcock shuts off the supply.
The ballcock prevents a cold water tank from overflowing.

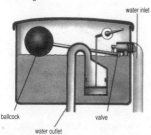

ballpoint pen   *noun*
A ballpoint pen is a kind of pen with a ball at its point. Ink flows from inside the pen over the surface of the ball and makes a mark when the pen is moved over the paper.
A ballpoint pen is smooth to write with.

bar code   *noun*
A bar code is a pattern of thick and thin lines with spaces between them. Bar codes are printed on the packages of goods in shops. They can be read by a **laser scanner** or light pen which passes the information to a **computer**.
Some libraries use bar codes to record the loan of books.

barometer   *noun*
A barometer is an instrument that measures atmospheric pressure. Atmospheric pressure is the weight of the air pressing down on the Earth. Barometers help us to forecast the weather.
The barometer shows that the pressure is lower than normal and it may rain.

BASIC   *noun*
BASIC is a **computer** language. The name BASIC comes from the initial letters of Beginner's All-purpose Symbolic Instruction Code.
This computer program is written in BASIC.

bathroom scales   *noun*
Bathroom scales are a **weighing machine**. People use them to check their weight. The weight is shown in kilograms on a dial that is read by the person standing on the platform of the scales.
The bathroom scales showed that he had gained one kilogram in one week.

bathyscaphe   *noun*
A bathyscaphe is an underwater vessel used by deep-sea explorers. It is made of thick, strong metals so that it can stand up to the strong pressures deep under the sea. A bathyscaphe can go as deep as 10,000 metres.
The scientists went down to the ocean floor in a bathyscaphe.

battery   *noun*
A battery is a device which supplies an **electric current**. It turns chemical energy into electrical energy. Some watches and calculators have tiny button batteries. Motor vehicles have large, powerful batteries.
There was no energy left in the batteries in her radio, so she bought new ones.

beam engine   *noun*

A beam engine is a machine that is used for pumping water. Its beam makes a see-saw motion when the engine is working. The beam connects the **piston** with the **pump** mechanism.

Beam engines were once used to pump water from coal mines.

beam scales   *noun*

Beam scales are a kind of **weighing machine**. They work like a see-saw. A pan hangs from each end of the beam. Objects placed in one pan are balanced against weights placed in the other.

The greengrocer weighed some apples on his beam scales.

bell ► **electric bell**

bevel gear   *noun*

A bevel gear is a device which has two **gear wheels**. They are set at an angle to each other. When the teeth move together, the direction of the driving force is changed from one angle to the other.

In a car, bevel gears change the direction of the driving force of the transmission shaft to the driving wheels.

bicycle   *noun*

A bicycle is a two-wheeled vehicle. Human feet pushing the pedals round provide the energy to drive a bicycle. It is steered by moving the handlebars.

The children rode their bicycles to school every day.

bimetal thermostat ► **thermostat**

binary digit   *noun*

A binary digit is a number. It is either 0 or 1. **Computers** use binary digits, or bits for short, for counting and passing on information.

All the information in a computer program is in binary digits.

binoculars ► page 21

bit ► **binary digit**

blast furnace   *noun*

A blast furnace is a special kind of **furnace**. It is used to take out, or extract, metal from metal ore. The ore is heated by an intense blast of air in the furnace, and oxygen and other **chemicals** are removed. The metal sinks to the bottom of the furnace.

Iron is obtained from iron ore in a blast furnace.

block and tackle   *noun*

A block and tackle is a kind of **pulley** system. It is used for lifting heavy weights. A length of rope or chain is wound two or more times between several pulleys and connected to the load to be lifted. The 'falls' of rope lessen the amount of effort needed.

We lifted the engine out of the boat by using a block and tackle.

boat   *noun*

A boat is a small **ship**. Boats can be powered by oars, sails or engines.

There was a race on the river between two rowing boats.

body scanner   *noun*

A body scanner is a machine used in hospitals to inspect a person's body for signs of disease. The scanner uses X-rays to build up pictures of the inside of the body. The pictures are shown on a screen.

The body scanner showed that the man was in very good health.

binoculars *noun*

Binoculars are a kind of **optical instrument**. They make an object seem nearer.

Binoculars contain **lenses** which increase, or magnify, the object's apparent size. The user looks through both eyepieces at the same time.

Through my binoculars I could see that the bird was a chaffinch.

magnified image

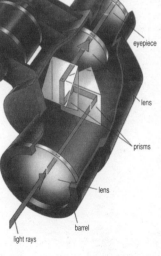

eyepiece

lens

prisms

lens

barrel

light rays

The cut-away section of a pair of binoculars shows the collection of lenses and prisms inside each barrel. Light rays from the object being viewed pass through the lenses which focus a magnified image onto the eyepiece. Two prisms fold, or concentrate, the light rays and turn the image the right way up for the eye. Looking through two barrels gives a three-dimensional image, like normal sight. Looking through the single barrel of a telescope gives a flat, two-dimensional image.

boiler *noun*
1. A boiler is a device which uses **fuel** to
boil water and make steam. The water runs
through tubes above the firebox which
contains the burning fuel. The steam is then
used in a **steam engine** or **steam turbine** to
provide power.
*A steam locomtoive is driven by steam
made in a boiler.*
2. A boiler is part of the central heating
system of a building. It heats water which is
stored in a metal tank. A pump sends the hot
water round the building.
*When they reached home, they found that
the boiler was not switched on, so there was
no heating in the house.*

bolt *noun*
A bolt is a kind of **simple machine** called a
screw. It is a metal rod which fastens two
things together. A spiral groove, called the
thread, runs round the shaft, or shank, of the
bolt. A **nut** twists onto this thread and can be
pulled tight using a **spanner**. The thread of
the nut slots together with the thread of the
bolt.
*A car engine is fixed tightly to the chassis
with bolts.*

boring machine ► **drill**

bottle opener *noun*
A bottle opener is a kind of **lever** that takes
the lid or cap off a bottle or jar. One end of
the bottle opener fits over the lid. Then the
lid is levered off by raising the other end of
the bottle opener.
*The children took a bottle opener with them
so that they could drink lemonade on their
picnic.*

bow-thruster *noun*
A bow-thruster is a device which helps some
ships to steer. It has two **propellers**
mounted on a shaft running across the bow
of the ship underwater.
*The liner was able to dock smoothly with the
help of its bow-thrusters.*

brace and bit
noun
A brace and bit is a
tool for making holes
in wood. The bit has
a sharp spiral at one
end. The other end is
fixed in the brace.
When the handle of
the brace is turned, a
bevel gear turns the
bit and cuts away a
circle of wood.
*He made a round hole
by using a brace and bit.*

brake *noun*
A brake is a device for making a machine,
such as an **automobile**, slow down or stop.
It works by rubbing against a brake shoe or
disc attached to the centre of one or more
wheels. This creates **friction** and causes the
machine to lose energy.
*The driver used the brake to stop at the
traffic lights.*

breath tester ► **alcohol breath tester**

bubblejet printer *noun*
A bubblejet printer is a kind of **printing
machine**. It is used to print documents
which have been typed on a word processor.
The bubblejet printer shoots tiny drops of
heated ink onto the paper.
*After he had typed the letter, he used a
bubblejet printer to print two copies.*

bulb ► **light bulb**

bullet *noun*
A bullet is an explosive device which sends
a small missile of metal or plastic from a
hand gun or rifle. The gun explodes a
charge in the body of the bullet, and this
shoots the bullet head towards its target at
enormous speed.
*The rifleman loaded his gun with a bullet,
aimed at the target and fired.*

burglar alarm *noun*

A burglar alarm is a device which gives a warning of unwanted intruders in a building. Some burglar alarms make bells or sirens ring. Others automatically send a message to the police. Modern burglar alarms have **sensors** which detect movement or body heat in a room.

The security guard heard the burglar alarm and went to see what was happening.

burner *noun*

A burner is the part of a heating or cooking device where fuel is set alight.

She turned on the gas and lit the burner of the cooker.

butane *noun*

Butane is a colourless gas. It can be turned into a liquid by compressing it. It can then be stored in a small container. Butane can be burnt as a fuel by releasing the pressure through a **valve**, which allows it to become a gas once again.

Liquid butane is stored in steel cylinders.

byte *noun*

A byte is a word used in computing. It means eight bits. The size of a computer's memory is measured in bytes, kilobytes or megabytes. A kilobyte is 1,000 bytes and a megabyte is 1,000,000 bytes.

The small computer had a memory of 64,000 bytes, or 64 kilobytes.

cable *noun*

A cable is a length of wires bundled together. Cables are usually made from **steel** or **copper**. Copper cables carry electricity and are often covered in plastic.

Cables bring electricity and telephone signals into our homes.

CAD ► computer-aided design

calculator *noun*

A calculator is a machine for counting quickly. It has number **keys** and function keys. When you press the number keys, information passes into the calculator. When you press the function keys, the calculator processes the information and the result is shown on the display panel.

If information is keyed in correctly, a calculator never makes a mistake.
calculate *verb*

cam *noun*

A cam is a kind of wheel which is not circular. It is used in machines to change circular movement into up and down movement.

Cams inside a car engine make the valves move up and down.

camera *noun*

A camera is a device for taking **photographs.** Light passes through **lenses** on to a **film** coated with chemicals which make the film sensitive to light. When the film is processed, we can see the pictures.

I used my camera to take photographs of the school sports.

camshaft *noun*
A camshaft is a steel rod with **cams**
attached to it. As a camshaft spins, the cams
raise and lower different parts of a machine.
*The camshaft turned four cams in the
engine.*

can opener *noun*
A can opener is a device for cutting through
the top of a can. Some can openers are
simple **levers** with a sharp point at one end
and a handle at the other. Others have a
sharp-edged wheel which is moved by a **cog
wheel**. A butterfly-shaped handle turns the
cog wheel.
*Some people have can openers fixed to the
wall of the kitchen.*

cantilever *noun*
A cantilever is a beam which is fixed at only
one end. Cantilevers can be used to span a
space where a support cannot be used.
*The bridge had two cantilevers which
stretched across the river.*

cantilever spring *noun*
A cantilever spring is a thin, flat strip of metal
fixed at one end. The other end is free to
move. After it has moved, it springs back
into its original position. For example, when
you press the button of an electric bell, a
cantilever spring connects an **electric
circuit** and makes the bell ring.
*Many electric gadgets contain a cantilever
axial spring.*

capacitor *noun*
A capacitor is a device for storing electricity.
It has layers made up of thin sheets of metal
which are separated by an **insulator**.
*Capacitors are used in the electric circuits of
radios, televisions and computers.*

car ► **automobile**

carbon arc lamp *noun*
A carbon arc lamp is a device which
produces a very bright light. An **electric
current** passes across the space between
two carbon rods. The rods become white hot
and glow very brightly.
*Some of the first carbon arc lamps were
used in lighthouses.*

carburettor *noun*
A carburettor is part of a **petrol engine**. It
mixes a fine spray of petrol with air. Inside
the engine, the mixture explodes and
releases energy.
*His car would not start because no petrol
was reaching the carburettor.*

cassette *noun*
A cassette is a plastic case containing
recording tape. Audio cassettes record
sound. Video cassettes can record sounds
and pictures. The tape's magnetic surface is
altered by **electric signals**.
*I listen to a cassette recording of my
favourite music.*

cast iron *noun*
Cast iron is a kind of **iron** made by pouring
molten iron into hollow moulds. It is dark
grey and breaks when dropped.
Domestic boilers are made of cast iron.

CAT scanner *noun*
A CAT scanner is a device which produces
X-ray images of any part of the body. It
scans the object from different angles and
produces a picture that doctors can study.
*The doctor thought that the patient had heart
disease and used a CAT scanner to find out.*

cat's eye *noun*

A cat's eye is a **device** which is set in rows along the surface of a road. It contains a glass reflector which reflects vehicle headlights at night.

It was foggy, but the cat's eyes helped the driver to keep to the correct side of the road.

catalytic converter *noun*

A catalytic converter is a **device** which can be fitted to the exhaust of a vehicle engine. It cuts down the amount of harmful gases released into the atmosphere. Catalytic converters contain metals which change the gases into less harmful ones.

Many countries have passed a law that all new cars must have a catalytic converter to reduce pollution.

cathode ray tube *noun*

A cathode ray tube is a glass tube which makes pictures from electronic signals. An **electron gun** inside the tube fires electrons at a screen. This makes the screen glow, and a picture is built up from tiny points of light.

A television screen is the screen at the end of a cathode ray tube.

CD-rom *noun*

CD-rom is a word which describes a method of storing information. CD is short for **compact disc** and rom is short for read-only memory. The database on a CD-rom can be read using a compact disc player and a **computer**.

A computer changes the information on a CD-rom into words which can be read on a screen.

central processing unit *noun*

A central processing unit, or CPU for short, is the part of a **computer** where the main work is done. It works on data that passes through it, using a **program**. The CPU then delivers the result to an **output**.

The central processing unit is the 'heart' of a computer.

centrifugal force *noun*

Centrifugal force is a **force** that acts on objects when they turn, or revolve. Centrifugal force tries to fling objects away from their central pivot point. The faster an object spins, the greater the centrifugal force.

The clothes in the spin drier were pushed outwards to the walls of the drum by centrifugal force.

centrifugal pump *noun*

A centrifugal pump is a **device** for separating liquids of different densities, such as **oil** and water. It spins the mixture, and the denser liquid, which is oil, is thrown to the sides.

Centrifugal pumps are used in dairies to separate milk from cream.

chain-saw *noun*

A chain-saw is a machine which is used for cutting wood. It has a chain of sharp-toothed links which is driven by a **petrol engine** or an **electric motor**.

The forester cut down the tree using a chain-saw.

chassis *noun*
A chassis is the frame on which a machine is built. The machine's parts are all attached to the chassis.
The automobile engine is bolted firmly onto the chassis.

checkout ► supermarket checkout

chemical *noun*
A chemical is a single substance which is pure. All living and non-living things are made of mixtures of chemicals.
Oxygen is a chemical in the air that we need to breathe to keep us alive.
chemical *adjective*

chimney *noun*
A chimney is a hollow pipe, usually made of brick or stone. It is connected to a fireplace, stove or furnace. The chimney creates a flow of air from its base above the fire, towards its top. This flow of air brings oxygen to the fire, and carries away the smoke and poisonous gases released by combustion.
The factory needed a tall chimney to draw enough air for the furnace.

chip ► silicon chip

chlorine *noun*
Chlorine is a yellow **gas** which dissolves in water. It is used in small quantities to make water safe to drink by killing harmful germs, or organisms.
They added chlorine to the water in the pool so it would be safe for swimming.

chromium *noun*
Chromium is a hard, silvery metal. It does not corrode. Chromium is often used to plate other metals, giving them a long-lasting, shiny finish. Chromium is mixed with iron to make stainless steel. This mixture of metals is called an **alloy**.
Many knives and forks are made from steel which contains chromium.

cinerama *noun*
Cinerama is a method of projecting motion pictures. Three separate pictures are projected onto a curved screen side by side. The three pictures make up one very wide picture.
Cinerama appears to put the audience right in the middle of the action of the film.

circuit board *noun*
A circuit board is a **device** which is part of an electronic appliance. It is a sheet of plastic covered with thin copper strips. These strips join together the parts, or components. A circuit board is sometimes called a printed circuit.
The mechanic made the computer work again by fitting a new circuit board.

circuit breaker *noun*
A circuit breaker is a kind of switch in an **electric circuit**. It **automatically** switches off the electricity if too much current flows into the circuit. You can reset a circuit breaker by putting the switch on again.
The circuit breaker cut off the electric current and all the lights went out.

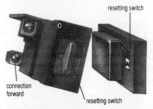

resetting switch

connection
forward

resetting switch

circular saw *noun*
A circular saw is a kind of machine for cutting wood or other materials. Its blade is like a **wheel**, with sharp teeth round the edge. A circular saw is powered by an **electric motor**. The saw is fixed on a cutting table, half above and half below the surface.
He cut the length of wood in half with a circular saw.

cistern *noun*

A cistern is a storage **tank**. Cisterns are used to store water to flush toilets and for baths and showers. When water is taken from them, they fill up again **automatically**. A ballcock controls the level of water.
While he was having a bath he could hear cold water refilling the cistern.

clamp *noun*

A clamp is a tool which holds things together so that work can be done on them. Some clamps work by tightening a **screw** or bolt. Others work by pressing a **lever**.
The clamp held the two pieces of wood together while the glue set.
clamp *verb*

clock *noun*

A clock is a machine for telling the time. Clocks can work either mechanically or electronically. Large mechanical clocks, such as **pendulum clocks**, are often driven by a weight. Smaller mechanical clocks are driven by small **springs** called mainsprings. An **analogue** clock has hands which move round a dial. A **digital** clock shows the time in figures.
She looked at the clock to check the time.

clockwork motor *noun*

A clockwork motor is a kind of machine. It stores **energy** in a circular **spring** which is wound up with a **key**. This energy is used to turn gear wheels. Clockwork motors are often used in toys.
The clock is driven by a clockwork motor.

gear wheels

key

main spring

clutch *noun*

A clutch is a part of a vehicle which is fitted between the **engine** and the **gearbox**. It has a rotating plate fixed to the engine and a similar one fixed to the gearbox shaft. Normally, they are pressed together by **springs**. A driver who wants to change gear presses a pedal to depress the clutch. This disconnects the engine from the gearbox. After the gear has been changed the clutch is connected, or engaged, again.
He depressed the clutch pedal and changed into top gear.

coal *noun*

Coal is a black, solid fossil made from the remains of trees and plants that died millions of years ago. Coal is mined underground, where it is found in layers, or seams. It is used in many parts of the world in power stations to produce steam for **turbines**, and for cooking and heating in homes. The two most important types of coal are hard coal, or anthracite, and soft or bituminous coal.
Coal is the fuel that is burned in steam locomotives.

coal face cutter ► page 28

coal gas *noun*

Coal gas is made when coal is heated in a closed space with no air. It is a mixture of **gases**, some of which are poisonous.
Coal gas is sometimes called town gas.

coal tar *noun*

Coal tar is a thick, black liquid. It is made when coal is burned and changes into coke. Coal tar contains many useful chemicals.
Coal tar is used in some disinfectants.

cobalt *noun*

Cobalt is a very hard and silvery metal. It is mixed with iron to make cobalt steel. This is used in the manufacture of hard cutting tools and drills.
The cobalt is mixed with molten iron inside the furnace.

27

coal face cutter *noun*

A coal face cutter is a machine for cutting
coal in a mine. Some cutters shear off slices
of coal and throw them onto a **conveyor
belt**. Others are like huge drills which work
along the side of the coal face.
*A modern coal face cutter can produce 800
tonnes of coal per hour.*

The cutting head of a coal face cutter can be adjusted
to cope with high or low layers, or seams, of coal.

cockpit *noun*

The cockpit of an aeroplane is where the pilot sits. It contains the instruments and controls. The cockpit of a large aeroplane is called the flight deck.
The pilot climbed into the cockpit and strapped himself in.

joystick

instrument panel

code *noun*

A code is a language made up of a group of signals, symbols, letters or numbers. The purpose of a code is to keep a message short or secret. In **computers**, codes are used as a method of storing or sending information. The binary code is the system of binary digits that computers use. A code of numbers is used to open a **combination lock**.
All information entered into computers is in code form.

coffee grinder *noun*

A coffee grinder chops coffee beans and turns them into ground coffee. It has a sharp blade which spins round inside a container. Most coffee grinders have electric motors. Some are operated by hand.
She put some beans in the coffee grinder to make fresh coffee for breakfast.

cog *noun*

A cog is a metal tooth on the outside edge of a gear wheel. The cogs on one gear fit, or mesh, together with the cogs on another.
The gear had 20 cogs round its outside edge.

cog wheel *noun*

A cog wheel is a wheel with **cogs** round its outside edge. The cogs on one cog wheel usually connect with the cogs on another.
In a watch with an **anchor escapement**, the teeth of the escapement connect with a cog wheel.
Cog wheels transfer energy from one part of a machine to another.

coil *noun*

1. A coil is a shape made when a length of wire, rope or other material is wound many times in a circle.
The sailors made coils of rope on the deck of the ship.
2. A coil is part of an **electric circuit**. It is a length of copper wire wound round an iron core. When electric current flows into it, the coil becomes an **electromagnet**.
Electric signals passing into the coil of a loudspeaker make the loudspeaker vibrate and produce sound.

coil spring *noun*

A coil spring is a length of metal formed into a **coil**. If the coil is squeezed together or pulled apart, it will return to its original shape once the squeezing force is removed. Coil springs are sometimes called helical springs.
There are coil springs inside the saddle of a bicycle.

coke *noun*

Coke is made when coal is burned to make **coal gas**. It is used in **blast furnaces** to help make **iron**.
Coke gives out very strong heat.

combination lock *noun*

A combination lock is a **lock** which does not need a **key**. It opens when a set of wheels are turned so that they show a number. This number is a **code** which is known only to the owner of the device to which the lock is fitted.
The manager knew the number which would open the safe's combination lock.

29

combine harvester ► page 32

combust verb
Combust is a word which means burn. When
something combusts, it combines with
oxygen and gives out heat **energy**.
*Ash is the waste product left behind when
wood combusts.*
combustion *noun*

combustion chamber *noun*
A combustion chamber is the sealed part of
a **furnace** where burning, or **combustion**,
takes place.
*Iron ore, limestone and coke were loaded
into the combustion chamber of the furnace.*

command *noun*
A command is an instruction to do
something. Commands can be given to a
computer by using a **keyboard**, a **mouse** or
a **joystick**.
*She gave the command to her computer to
print her poem.*
command *verb*

communications *noun*
Communications are ways of sending
messages between living things or between
machines. When we talk or write to
someone, we are using communications.
Telecommunications are communications
using **electronics**.
*The telephone allows us to communicate
with people over long distances.*

commutator *noun*
A commutator is a part of some **electric
motors** and **generators**. When it revolves
inside the fixed part of the machine, an
electric current is generated.
*The commutator spins round inside the
electric motor.*

compact disc *noun*
A compact disc is a thin, plastic disc which
contains **digital** information. It is often used
for music recordings, but can also carry
other kinds of information.
*Her birthday present was a compact disc of
her favourite singer.*

compass *noun*
A compass is an instrument which helps to
show in which direction someone or
something is travelling. A magnetic compass
contains a magnet in the shape of a needle.
The ends of the needle always point to
magnetic north and south.
*The sailors used a compass to point their
way to the north.*

compressed air *noun*
Compressed air is air that has been
squeezed into a small space. This increases
its pressure. When compressed air is
released, it returns to normal atmospheric
pressure with force. This force can be used
as a source of **energy**.
*In a car factory, car bodies are sprayed with
paint by using compressed air.*

compressor *noun*

A compressor is a machine for squeezing air or other gases into a small space. It is powered by a **motor** using **electricity**, **oil** or **petrol**.
The road-menders used air tools which were powered by a compressor.

computer *noun*

A computer is an electronic machine which can assess information very quickly. Information is given to the computer through an **input**. When the computer has finished the task, it presents the results on an **output**. This is usually a visual display unit or a print-out.
I used my computer to work out how much my holiday would cost.

computer-aided design *noun*

Computer-aided design, or CAD for short, is a way of designing objects with the help of a **computer**. The designer can see on a VDU screen how an object will look and behave when it is built.
Computer-aided design is used to design cars, ships, structures and machines.

concave lens *noun*

A concave lens is a piece of ground glass. It is thicker at the edges than in the middle. Concave lenses make rays of light spread out. They are used in **movie projectors**.
He used a slide projector with a concave lens to shine the picture on the wall.

concrete mixer *noun*

A concrete mixer is a machine which mixes sand, gravel, water and cement together. It mixes them in a revolving drum driven by a **motor**. Concrete is used in building work.
The builders used a concrete mixer to make concrete for the path.

condenser *noun*

1. A condenser is a device for storing **electricity**. It is often called a **capacitor**.
The condenser fitted to the car's engine releases a spark to ignite the fuel.
2. A condenser is part of the equipment used to change a gas into a liquid.
The condenser cools the gas to make the change.

control panel *noun*

A control panel is a display of instruments which shows how a machine is performing. The instruments show things such as the machine's speed and temperature.
The control panel of a motor car is called the dashboard or facia.

control surfaces *noun*

Control surfaces are parts of an **aircraft**. They can be made to move by the pilot to control the direction of the plane. The **ailerons** along the trailing edge of the wings tilt the aircraft left or right. The **rudder** on top of the tail plane turns the aircraft left or right. The elevators at the base of the tail plane make the aircraft climb or dive.
The pilot turned the aircraft by moving the control surfaces.

control tower ► page 34

control unit *noun*

A control unit is a **device** which is part of a machine. The operator of the machine presses buttons or moves **levers** on the control unit to make the machine perform a task.
Pressing buttons on a lift's control unit makes the lift go up or down.

combine harvester *noun*

A combine harvester is a large farm machine
that cuts cereal crops, separates the grain
and throws out the stalks and husks.
*Using a combine harvester, the farmer was
able to finish the harvest in one day.*

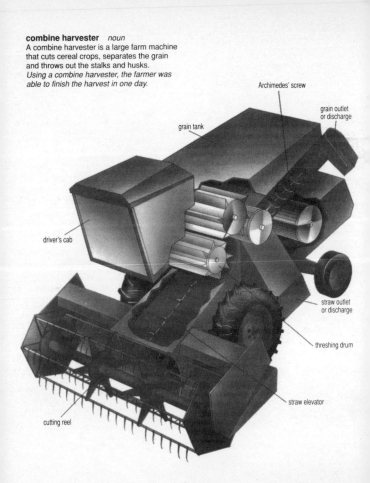

Archimedes' screw

grain outlet
or discharge

grain tank

driver's cab

straw outlet
or discharge

threshing drum

straw elevator

cutting reel

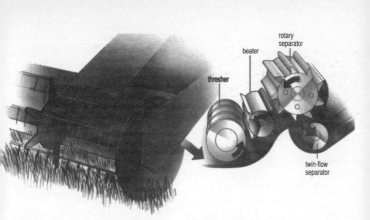

thresher

beater

rotary separator

twin-flow separator

The height of a combine harvester's cutting reel can be changed to cut crops of different lengths.

The crop is threshed and the grain separated in four stages, using four different kinds of drum or rotor.

The separated grain flows through the discharge pipe into a container called a grain pot. An Archimedes' screw inside the pipe keeps the grain flowing.

control tower *noun*

A control tower is a tall building at an airport.
People called air traffic controllers work
there. They give instructions to pilots, telling
them when it is safe to taxi, take off or land
their aircraft.
*There is a good view of the runways from
the airport control tower.*

convex lens   *noun*
A convex lens is a piece of ground glass. It is thick in the middle and thin at the edges. A convex lens concentrates light passing through it onto a focal point.
There are convex lenses in cameras and binoculars.

conveyor   *noun*
A conveyor is a machine which carries things automatically from one place to another. It has an endless moving belt made of steel, rubber or plastic. Conveyors carry machine parts in assembly plants, luggage at airports and coal in mines.
The parts of the engine were bolted on as it travelled along on the conveyor.

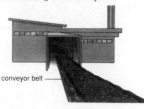
conveyor belt

coolant   *noun*
A coolant is a liquid which is used to take away excess heat in a machine. The heat produced by an **engine** is drawn off through waterways and pipes close to the moving parts. When metal is being cut on a **lathe**, a special oil and water mixture is sprayed on the cutting tool to stop it becoming too hot.
Water is used as a coolant in most car engines.

cooling system   *noun*
A cooling system is part of an engine. It is made up of a **pump** which pumps a coolant through pipes and waterways close to the engine's working parts to cool them.
The car engine overheated because there was a fault in the cooling system.

cooling tower   *noun*
A cooling tower is part of a power station. It is made of concrete. Hot water from the turbines sprays down inside the cooling tower. The cold air in the tower cools the hot water. Some water is given off as water vapour from the top of the tower.
We were a long way away from the power station, but we could see its cooling towers.

copper   *noun*
Copper is a **chemical** element. It is a soft, reddish-brown metal. Copper is a very good conductor of heat and electricity. It is used to make pipes and electric wires. When copper is mixed with other metals, it makes **alloys**, such as bronze and brass.
The electrical circuits in a house are made of copper wire covered with plastic.

counterweight   *noun*
A counterweight is a weight used to balance the weight of a moving part in a machine. It can be used to balance the weight of the moving part, so that its movement can be easily controlled. The counterweights in a sash window make it easier to raise or lower.
A counterweight in a lift shaft balances the weight of the lift.

CPU ► **central processing unit**

crane   *noun*
A crane is a machine for lifting and moving heavy loads. Some cranes are fixed to the ground. Others move along rails, hang from **gantries** or are mounted on **vehicles**.
The crane lifted the car onto the back of the breakdown truck.

crank   *noun*
A crank is a part of a machine. It is a **shaft** bent at right angles. A crank converts to-and-fro motion into circular motion.
The crank of a bicycle turns the up-and-down movement of the knees into circular motion.

crankshaft   *noun*
A crankshaft is part of an **internal combustion engine**. It is a thick, steel rod bent at right angles, to which the **pistons** are connected. When the pistons move up and down, the crankshaft turns, or revolves.
The starter motor turned the crankshaft to start the car's engine.

crawler   *noun*
A crawler is a device for inspecting the underneath of machines. It is a trolley low enough to be wheeled under the machine with a person lying flat on it.
The mechanic used a crawler to see what was wrong with the lorry.

crop sprayer   *noun*
A crop sprayer is a **device** for spraying water, fertilizers or pesticides onto growing farm crops. It has a tank containing liquid, a **pump**, and a nozzle which makes a fine spray. Crop sprayers are hand-held, pulled by tractor, or attached to small aircraft.
The farmer used a crop sprayer to kill the aphids which had attacked his beans.

crude oil ► **petroleum**

cut-out   *noun*
A cut-out is a **device** which **automatically** cuts off electricity or the fuel supply to a machine. It works if there is an emergency or if the machine has developed a fault. Some cut-outs work electronically to operate switches. Others work by springs and wires.
When the engine became too hot, the cut-out shut it down.

cutting machine   *noun*
A cutting machine is a device for cutting and shaping metal. It is fitted with sharp cutting tools. Some cutting machines cut across the metal. Others cut it from above.
The mechanic shaped a new cover for the engine with a cutting machine.

cylinder   *noun*
A cylinder is part of a machine. It is a hollow tube with a **piston** which moves up and down inside it. Pressure placed inside the cylinder makes the piston move.
Many motor cars have four-cylinder engines.
cylindrical   *adjective*

D

dairy machines ► page 38

daisy-wheel printer *noun*
A daisy-wheel printer is a device which is used with a computer. It produces a printed **output**.
Each spoke of a daisy-wheel printer's wheel carries a different print character.

dashboard *noun*
A dashboard is a part of the inside of a motor car. It lies in front of the driver.
The dashboard has instruments which record the car's speed, the amount of fuel left, and other information.

data *plural noun*
Data is a plural word which means information. Computers receive data from a disk, magnetic tape or other **input**. They can store the data and process it.
People and computers use data to solve problems and answer questions.

database *noun*
A database is a collection of information. It can be stored on a **disk** or **magnetic tape**, or in the memory of a **computer**. The computer can find each piece of information very quickly.
The club stored the names and addresses of all its members on a database.

deflector *noun*
A deflector is a part of a machine which changes the direction of material striking it.
Deflectors are often used to make sure that waste material is put in the right place.

derailleur gear *noun*
Derailleur gear is a set of **gears** on a **bicycle**. It is used to make the most of the power delivered to a bicycle's rear wheel by the cyclist. A derailleur gear has a number of **gear wheels** which are brought into action by moving a control lever.
Her bicycle had derailleur gears, and so she was able to reach the top of the hill first.

derrick *noun*
A derrick is a kind of **crane**. It raises or lowers an object above a fixed point.
Derricks are used on oil exploration rigs to drill for oil.

desalination *noun*
Desalination is the removal of salt from sea water. Equipment for doing this is called desalination **plant**. There are a number of different ways of desalinating salt water. Water that has been desalinated is suitable for drinking.
The ship's lifeboats were fitted with desalination plant.
desalinate *verb*

device *noun*
A device is a small, manufactured object which is designed for a special purpose.
Locks, **switches** and lamps are all different kinds of device.
A meter is a device for showing measurements.

dairy machines *noun*

Dairy machines are pieces of equipment which treat, or process, cow's milk. Some machines milk the cows. Some machines treat the milk to make it completely safe. Other machines remove the cream to make skimmed milk. Others put the milk into bottles or cartons and seal them.
Milk from the farm is processed in dairy machines.

A milking parlour

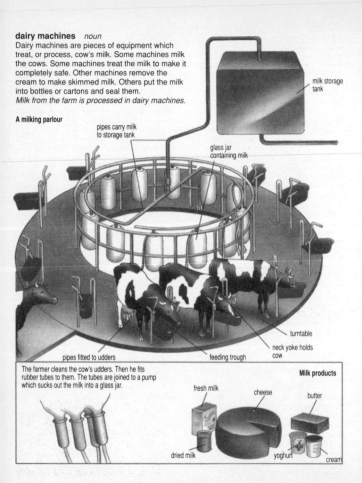

milk storage tank

pipes carry milk to storage tank

glass jar containing milk

turntable

neck yoke holds cow

pipes fitted to udders

feeding trough

The farmer cleans the cow's udders. Then he fits rubber tubes to them. The tubes are joined to a pump which sucks out the milk into a glass jar.

Milk products

fresh milk

cheese

butter

dried milk

yoghurt

cream

38

dial *noun*

A dial is a **device** which is used on many measuring instruments. It usually has a round face like a clock. A hand or needle on the dial points to measurements marked round the outside.
The dial of the speedometer showed how fast the car was travelling.

diaphragm *noun*

A diaphragm is a thin, flat sheet of metal, rubber or plastic. When a **force** pushes against a diaphragm, it moves. In a **loudspeaker**, a diaphragm changes **electric signals** into sounds as it vibrates.
A diaphragm in a telephone changes signals coming down the wire into sounds.

diaphragm pump *noun*

A diaphragm pump is a **device** for pumping gases or liquids. It uses a **diaphragm** to make a **vacuum**. The gas or liquid is drawn into the pump by the vacuum and pushed out, or expelled, by moving the diaphragm in the opposite direction. A **diaphragm valve** keeps the flow moving in the right direction.
A bicycle pump is a diaphragm pump which draws in air from outside and pushes it into the tyre.

diaphragm valve *noun*

A diaphragm valve is a **device** which allows a liquid or gas to pass in only one direction. The diaphragm fits loosely across an opening to allow the liquid or gas to pass, but closes tightly to stop it escaping.
The human heart has a type of diaphragm valve to keep the blood flowing.

die-casting *noun*

Die-casting is a way of forming metal. The metal is heated until it is molten. Then it is poured into a mould called a die. Die-casting is used to produce rough articles that must be finished by hand or machine before use. The dies can be used again and again.
Die-casting allowed them to produce hundreds of model soldiers in a day.

diesel engine *noun*

A diesel engine is a kind of **internal combustion engine**. It burns a mixture of air and **diesel fuel** to produce **energy**. The mixture is ignited by the heat produced by compression instead of by a **spark plug**. The diesel engine was patented by a German inventor called Rudolf Diesel.
Diesel engines are often used to generate electricity at a fairground.

diesel fuel *noun*

Diesel fuel is a liquid made from **oil**. It is used as a **fuel** for **diesel engines**. Another name for diesel fuel is DERV, which is short for Diesel Engine Road Vehicle.
He filled the truck's tanks with diesel fuel.

differential *noun*

A differential is a system of **gears** which allows parts of a **machine** to move at different speeds. The differential in an **automobile** lets the driving wheels move at different speeds when rounding corners.
The differential allows the outside wheel to travel further and faster than the inside wheel.

digger *noun*

A digger is a large machine for making holes and trenches in the ground. It is a kind of **tractor** which digs a shovel-shaped tool into the ground. The digging arm is powered by **hydraulics**.
The gang used a digger to make a trench for the new water pipes.

digital *adjective*

Digital describes the use of numbers for any purpose. A digital **watch** shows the time in numbers. An **analogue** watch shows the time by hands which move round a dial.

The numbers 0 and 1 are digital numbers which computers use to make calculations.

digit *noun*

digital audio tape *noun*

Digital audio tape, or DAT for short, is magnetic tape which contains recorded **electric signals**. These can be fed into a digital player and changed back into sound signals. Recordings made on digital audio tape are of a very high quality.

She gave her brother a new tape player which used digital audio tape.

direct current *noun*

Direct current, or DC for short, is a kind of electric current. It flows through an electric circuit in only one direction. **Batteries** send direct current to the devices for which they provide power. The opposite of direct current is **alternating current**.

A battery produces direct current for a flashlight.

disc *noun*

A disc is a round, thin, flat object. A **compact disc** is a kind of disc used to record and play back sound.

He put a compact disc on the turntable of the record-player and they listened to the music.

disc brakes *noun*

Disc brakes are used to slow down or stop a machine. A disc is attached to the machine's moving parts. Pads push against the disc to stop the machine by creating **friction**. In an **automobile**, disc brakes are attached to the hubs of the wheels and slow them down.

She applied the disc brakes and brought her car to a stop.

disc drive ► **disk drive**

dish antenna *noun*

A dish antenna is a kind of **aerial**. It has a curved shape like a dish. A dish antenna collects radio signals and passes them to a **receiver**. Dish antennae that are made to receive radio signals from the stars may be up to 300 metres across.

The dish antenna on our house allows us to receive satellite television programmes.

dishwasher *noun*

A dishwasher is an electrical **appliance** which cleans dirty pots, pans and cutlery. It rinses, washes and then dries them. A dishwasher is powered by an **electric motor**.

After the party, we put all the pans and plates into the dishwasher.

disk ► **floppy disk and hard disk**

disk drive *noun*

A disk drive is part of a **computer**. It collects data from the **hard** or the **floppy disks** and passes it to the **central processing unit**.

He put a floppy disk into the computer's disk drive.

distillation *noun*

Distillation is a process which makes liquids pure by boiling them. Pure vapour rises from the boiling liquid. When the vapour is collected and cooled, it turns into a pure liquid, or condenses.

Car batteries use water that has been made pure by distillation.

dot matrix printer *noun*

A dot matrix printer is a device which is often used for the **output** of a **computer**. It has a print head which contains a number of needles. These print characters by making ink dots on the paper.

She used a dot matrix printer to print the work she had done on her computer.

dredger *noun*

A dredger is a kind of **ship**. It clears mud and sand from the beds of harbours so that they are deep enough for other ships to use. The mud is collected by a chain of large shovels and then taken away to be dumped.

The dredger was hard at work because the storm had made a sandbank in the harbour.

drill *noun*

A drill is a tool for making holes. The part of the drill that cuts the hole is made from a hard **steel** and is called the bit. It has two special grooves cut into it which make it look like a large screw. The edges of the grooves, or spiros, are very sharp. Drills are used by carpenters, metal-workers, road-builders and workers on oil rigs.

He drilled holes in the two metal parts so that he could bolt them together.

drill *verb*

drive cog *noun*

A drive cog is part of a machine. It is the **gear** that turns the working parts of the machine.

When the machine was working, the drive cog turned a shaft which made the wheels turn.

drive shaft *noun*

A drive shaft is a steel rod. It is part of a machine. The drive shaft sends, or transmits, power from the **engine** to the moving parts of the machine.

The car's drive shaft connected with the gears of the rear axle and made it turn.

driving gears *noun*

Driving gears are a set of **gears** which make the most of the power delivered to a vehicle's wheels by the **engine**.

Most cars have four or five driving gears.

drop hammer *noun*

A drop hammer is a large tool used in an iron foundry. It has a heavy head which is dropped onto red-hot iron to beat it into shape.

The men wore ear-muffs to protect their ears from the noise of the drop hammer.

drum brake *noun*

A drum brake is a **device** for slowing down or stopping a vehicle or machine. A steel drum is fixed to the hubs of the wheels and revolves with them. Pads or shoes made of **asbestos** push out against the inside of the drum to cause **friction** and slow it down.

Most old cars have drum brakes.

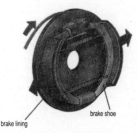

brake shoe

brake lining

41

dynamo *noun*
A dynamo is a machine for **generating electricity**. It has a shaft wound with copper wire which spins inside a **magnet**. This makes electricity flow into an electric circuit.
My bicycle has a dynamo which lights its front and rear lamps.

dynamometer *noun*
A dynamometer is an instrument for measuring **energy**. It is used to test how well a machine works.
The engineers tested the power of the new engine with a dynamometer.

E

earphones *noun*
Earphones are an electrical **device** which allows one person to listen to sounds without disturbing other people. They fit inside the ear. They work just like a telephone **receiver**.
My brother was doing his homework, so I listened to records on my earphones.

earth drill *noun*
An earth drill is a tool for making holes in the ground. Some earth drills are shaped like a flat-bladed **corkscrew** and are small enough for one or two men to turn by hand. Other earth drills are power operated and may be as large as a train. These very large earth drills are used for tunnelling. They have many rotating cutting blades.
They dug for oil with an earth drill.

egg whisk ► whisk

electric bell *noun*
An electric bell is a **device** which gives a warning. When the button is pressed, an **electric current** and a magnet make a small hammer vibrate against the metal bell case. This makes a ringing sound.
She rang the electric bell to let her friend know that she had arrived.

electric cable *noun*
An electric cable is a bundle of long wires which carry **electric current**. The wires are usually made of **copper** and covered with **plastic** to **insulate** the cable.
They dug a trench to take the electric cable to the new house.

electric circuit   *noun*
An electric circuit is a never-ending path along which **electric current** flows. It is usually made of wires which link the source of **electricity** to **appliances**. Most electric circuits have **switches** so that they can be turned on or off.
A ring main is an electric circuit which links up all the power points in a house.

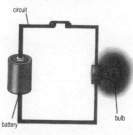

electric current   *noun*
An electric current is a flow of **electricity**. It is made when **electrons** flow through an **electric circuit**. An electric current can be **alternating** or **direct**.
The on-off switch controls the flow of electric current through a radio.

electric drill   *noun*
An electric drill is a tool for making holes. It is powered by an **electric motor**. Dentists use small electric drills to remove tooth decay.
He used an electric drill to make a hole in the wall.

electric generator   *noun*
An electric generator is a machine which makes **electricity**. It uses **coal**, water, **oil** or **nuclear** material as fuel. A generator can produce either **direct current** or **alternating current**.
Electric generators are found at power stations.

electric guitar   *noun*
An electric guitar is a musical instrument. It is played by plucking the strings. An electric guitar is connected to an **amplifier** which makes it sound louder.
Two of the musicians in the group played electric guitars.

electric horn   *noun*
An electric horn is a **device** which is fitted to a vehicle. When the button is pressed, a **diaphragm** vibrates and the horn gives a loud warning.
The driver sounded the electric horn to warn the children playing in the road.

electric mixer   *noun*
An electric mixer is an **appliance** used in cooking. It contains an **electric motor**. The motor turns a blade or whisk which mixes up the ingredients of the dish that is being made.
She put flour and margarine into the electric mixer and switched it on.

electric motor   ► page 44

electric signal   *noun*
An electric signal is a kind of message produced by electricity. Electric signals flow through a **television** set when it is switched on. They allow us to see the picture and hear the sound.
The loudspeaker changes electric signals into sound waves.

electric motor   *noun*

An electric motor is a **device** which changes electrical energy into **kinetic energy**. It uses **electric current** which turns a **drive shaft**. *The electric motor in a vacuum cleaner turns a fan which sucks up dust.*

Electric trains, such as the French TGV, are powered by electric motors. Electricity is picked up by the motor from an overhead cable or from a third rail running beside the usual pair of rails.

electric storage batteries

Electric road vehicles, such as this delivery van, are quiet and do not pollute the atmosphere. But they are slow and cannot travel very far, so can only be used for short journeys in towns and cities.

electric motor

air in to cool motor

air out

Electric motors are used to drive many kinds of machine tool, such as this lathe.

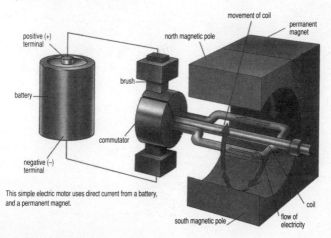

positive (+) terminal

battery

negative (−) terminal

north magnetic pole

brush

commutator

movement of coil

permanent magnet

coil

flow of electricity

south magnetic pole

This simple electric motor uses direct current from a battery, and a permanent magnet.

electricity *noun*
Electricity is a kind of **energy**. It can be produced by **batteries** or made in a **power station**. Electricity is used to light lamps and power electric tools and appliances. Electricity occurs naturally in thunder storms.
Many people have cookers in their homes which work by electricity.

electrode *noun*
An electrode is part of an electric **battery**. A battery has two electrodes. **Electric current** flows from the positive electrode into a circuit and returns to the negative electrode. On the outside of a battery, the positive electrode is marked with a plus sign and the negative electrode with a minus sign.
It is important to fit a battery into a torch with the electrodes the right way round.

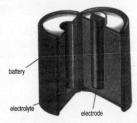

battery

electrolyte

electrode

electrolysis *noun*
Electrolysis is a process in which **electricity** makes chemical changes happen. When electricity flows through certain liquids, it causes new substances to form.
Chlorine gas is produced from salt by electrolysis.

electromagnet *noun*
An electromagnet is a coil of wire wound round an iron rod. When an **electric current** passes through the wire, the rod becomes magnetic.
Many electrical appliances, such as electric motors, contain electromagnets.

electron *noun*
An electron is a tiny particle of matter. There are electrons in all the atoms which make up everything in the universe. An **electric current** is made up of moving electrons.
Electrons cannot be seen even with the most powerful microscope.

electron gun *noun*
An electron gun is part of a **television receiver**. It uses **electricity** to fire a stream of **electrons** at a screen. The electrons move very quickly and make up the picture on the screen.
The electron gun is at the back of the television set.

electron microscope *noun*
An electron microscope is an instrument which makes very small objects look larger, or magnifies them. It contains an **electron gun** which is aimed at the object to be magnified. The image is shown on a screen.
An electron microscope can magnify objects up to one million times.

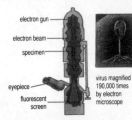

electron gun

electron beam

specimen

eyepiece

fluorescent screen

virus magnified 190,000 times by electron microscope

electronic *adjective*
Electronic describes **devices** which use streams of **electrons** to make them work. **Radios**, **televisions** and **computers** are all electronic devices.
Television engineers study electronic engineering as part of their training.

electronics *noun*

46

electronic calculator   *noun*
An electronic calculator is a **device** for making quick, accurate calculations. It has a **keypad** on which numbers and instructions can be given. When these are keyed in, the answer then appears on a display panel.
Many electronic calculators contain batteries.

electronic flash   *noun*
An electronic flash is a **device** fitted to some **cameras**. It operates a flash bulb which lights up when a photograph is taken. An electronic flash is needed when there is not enough natural light. It is powered by a **battery**.
He used an electronic flash at night.

electronic point of sale ► EPOS

electronic signals ► electric signals

electroplating   *noun*
Electroplating is a process which coats one metal with a thin layer of another metal. The metals are put into a solution which carries an **electric current**. The current makes a thin layer of one metal form on the other. Chromium is a tough but expensive metal. It is used to electroplate the surface of a cheap metal, such as iron, which rusts.
Electroplating is used to make silver-plated table cutlery.
electroplate   *verb*

electrostatic painting   *noun*
Electrostatic painting is a process used to paint motor car bodies. The car body and a spray gun are given a negative and a positive electric charge. The paint completes an **electric circuit** as it is sprayed onto the metal.
Electrostatic painting gives a car body an even coat of paint.

electrostatic precipitator   *noun*
An electrostatic precipitator is a machine which removes solid particles from smoke. It passes the smoke through a network of wires which carry an **electric current**. The solid particles become electrically charged and are attracted onto collecting plates.
An electrostatic precipitator helps to cut down pollution that is caused by factory smoke.

enamelling   *noun*
Enamelling is a process that covers metal with a hard, glass-like coating. It is used for decoration and to protect metal from corrosion. The metal surface of the object is covered with a wet powder of enamel. It is then heated to a very high temperature so that the enamel melts and sticks to the surface of the metal.
Enamelling protected the case of the instruments from the weather.

endoscope   *noun*
An endoscope is an instrument for viewing the internal parts of the body. It is used to detect diseases. It contains a tiny television camera that can be placed inside the body.
The doctor used an endoscope to examine the patient's stomach.
endoscopy   *noun*

engine   *noun*
An engine is a machine which uses **energy** from fuel to perform tasks. **Steam engines** and **internal combustion engines** are two kinds of engine.
A racing car has a very powerful engine.

epicyclic gears   *noun*

Epicyclic gears are parts of some machines. They consist of two **gear wheels**, one small and the other larger. The smaller gear fits into the larger and turns round inside it. Large gears turn more slowly than smaller ones.
Some cars are fitted with epicyclic gears.

EPOS   *noun*

EPOS stands for electronic point of sale. It describes a system used at the **tills** of some shops. EPOS devices record each sale and automatically re-order supplies of the goods which have been purchased.
The new supermarket is fitted with EPOS checkouts.

escalator   *noun*

An escalator is a moving staircase. It is powered by an **electric motor**. The stairs are made of metal and are hinged together to make an endless belt, for carrying passengers up or down
We used the escalator to travel from the underground station platform to the street.

escape wheel   *noun*

An escape wheel is a part of the **anchor escapement** of a watch or clock. It is a toothed wheel. As the anchor rocks backwards and forwards, it catches and turns one tooth of the wheel at a time.
The ticking sound of a clock is made by the movements of the escape wheel.

escapement clock   *noun*

An escapement clock is a clock with a **spring** mechanism which is wound with a **key**. The **energy** which pushes the hands round is stored in the spring and allowed to escape a little at a time.
Her escapement clock has not worked for some time because she has lost the key.

etching   *noun*

Etching is a way of making designs on metal. It is done in two ways. One method is to use a sharp instrument to cut into the metal. The other is to cover the metal with wax which is cut away from the parts to be etched. The metal is then placed in acid, which eats the uncovered parts away.
Etching is sometimes used to make plates from which pictures are printed.

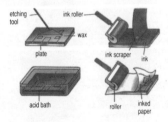

evaporator   *noun*

An evaporator is part of a **refrigerator** or **freezer**. It is a **coil** into which a liquid called freon is pumped at high pressure. As the liquid enters the evaporator, its pressure drops. As the pressure drops, the liquid turns into a gas which takes in, or absorbs, heat from inside the refrigerator. All liquids absorb heat as they evaporate. In the process, any food or liquid that has been stored in the refrigerator loses heat. This keeps stored poducts fresh.
The evaporator in a freezer is sometimes called the cooling coil.

excavator   *noun*

An excavator is a machine for digging. It is
powered by a **diesel engine**. An excavator
is fitted with a long arm which has a metal
shovel at the end. The driver can control the
movements of the shovel from the cab by
using **hydraulic rams**.
*The excavator was digging the foundations
for a new road.*

exhaust ► **exhaust gas**

exhaust gas   *noun*

Exhaust gas is the mixture of waste gases
which comes out of the exhaust pipe of an
engine. A **steam engine** produces steam as
its exhaust gas. The exhaust gas from
internal combustion engines is poisonous.
It includes carbon monoxide, nitrogen oxide
and lead.
*There was a great deal of traffic and the air
was full of exhaust gas.*

exploration rig   *noun*

An exploration or drilling rig is a kind of **oil
rig**. It is a structure used in the search for
oil. An exploration rig is a tall metal tower
which supports a drill. Exploration rigs used
at sea are built on platforms. They also have
living quarters for the workers and a place
for helicopters to land.
*News came from the exploration rig that oil
had been discovered.*

extrudor   *noun*

An extrudor is a part of a machine. It forms
metal, plastics or artificial fibres into shapes.
An extrudor squirts the material out of a
nozzle.
*Nylon is made by mixing chemicals and
pushing the mixture through an extrudor.*

F

facia ► **dashboard**

facsimile ► **fax**

fan   *noun*

A fan is an **appliance** for keeping things or
people cool. It has a number of blades fixed
to a shaft which is turned by a **motor**. Fans
that are used in buildings are powered by
electricity.
*Most car engines have a fan which cools the
water in the radiator.*

fax   *noun*

Fax is short for facsimile. It is a written
message sent by telephone. A fax machine
copies a document placed in it and sends
electric signals to another fax machine.
This produces a copy of the document.
*He sent a fax in three minutes from London
to New York.*
fax   *verb*

ferrous   *adjective*

Ferrous is a word which describes **iron**, or
any metal containing iron. Ferrous metals
are alloys which contain large amounts of
iron. They can be picked up by a magnet
because magnets attract iron.
*Steel is made from iron and so it is a ferrous
metal.*

ferry   *noun*

A ferry is a kind of **ship**. It carries
passengers and vehicles across rivers,
canals or narrow stretches of sea.
*We took the car by ferry from England to
France.*

fibre optics ► page 51

fibreglass   *noun*
Fibreglass is a strong and very lightweight material made by weaving threads of spun glass. It is sometimes used for curtains and for covering furniture.
Some boat hulls and car bodies are made from fibreglass, mixed with plastics.

file   *noun*
1. A file is a tool, made of hardened metal. It is used to shape wood or metal. It has a rough surface with a diamond-shaped pattern cut into it.
He used a file to shape the metal so that it fitted exactly into the hole.
2. A file is information stored on a computer **disk** or in the computer's **memory**. Every file has a name so it can be found easily.
I am starting some new work on my computer and have opened a new file.

film   *noun*
1. A film is a thin layer of a solid or a liquid. In machines, a film of **oil** is spread over the working parts as a **lubricant**.
There was a film of oil on top of the water.
2. A film is a strip of material called celluloid. It is coated with **chemicals** which change when light falls on them. **Cameras** and **movie cameras** use film to take **photographs** and make movies.
He loaded a new film into his camera.

filter   *noun*
1. A filter is a **device** which separates liquids or gases. Tiny holes in the filter allow the liquid or gas to pass through. Solids are left behind in the filter.
A car's air filter removes dust from the air entering the engine.
2. A filter is a **disc** of coloured glass or plastic. It takes in, or absorbs, different colours from light. Photographers sometimes fit filters over the **lenses** of their **cameras**.
A red filter allows only the colour red to pass through it.

fire appliance   *noun*
A fire appliance is a vehicle used by fire-fighters. Some fire appliances carry a supply of water. Others have turntable ladders and other equipment. Fire appliances are sometimes called fire engines.
The fire-fighters arrived in three fire appliances.

fire detector   *noun*
A fire detector is a **sensor** device for giving a warning if fire breaks out. It may sense heat or smoke. It sounds a siren or a bell.
We left the building because the fire detector sounded the alarm.

fire engine ► **fire appliance**

fire extinguisher   *noun*
A fire extinguisher is a **device** for putting out a fire. It sprays water, chemicals or foam on the flames, putting them out by cutting off their oxygen supply and cooling the burning material.
He sprayed foam from the fire extinguisher onto the flames.

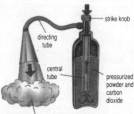
strike knob
directing tube
central tube
pressurized powder and carbon dioxide
carbon dioxide smothers fire

fire-fighting ► page 52

flight deck   *noun*
A flight deck is the part of an **aircraft** where the controls are found.
The pilot and co-pilot sat on the flight deck.

flight simulator ► page 54

fibre optics *noun*

Fibre optics is a way of sending messages
by light waves. The messages travel along
thin fibres made of glass. Special equipment
turns the **electric signals** which make up
the messages into flickers, or pulses, of light.
*Fibre optics are often used instead of copper
cables for carrying telephone messages.*

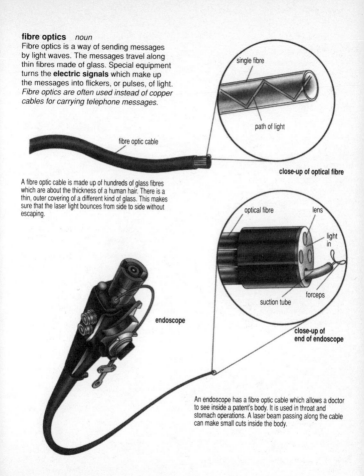

single fibre

path of light

close-up of optical fibre

fibre optic cable

A fibre optic cable is made up of hundreds of glass fibres
which are about the thickness of a human hair. There is a
thin, outer covering of a different kind of glass. This makes
sure that the laser light bounces from side to side without
escaping.

optical fibre

lens

light
in

forceps

suction tube

**close-up of
end of endoscope**

endoscope

An endoscope has a fibre optic cable which allows a doctor
to see inside a patent's body. It is used in throat and
stomach operations. A laser beam passing along the cable
can make small cuts inside the body.

fire-fighting *verb*
Fire-fighting describes the work of putting out
fires. Many different machines and other
kinds of equipment are used.
Fire-fighting is sometimes dangerous work.

An elevating platform truck can lift fire-
fighters up to spray water onto very tall
buildings. Hydraulic rams raise the boom
with the platform on the end.

water nozzle

platform

boom

hydraulic ram

turntable

portable ladders

storage compartment

jack

Temperatures at which materials burn

paper
232°C

cotton
266°C

cellophane 242°

wood
190°C

gas
432°C

Steam pumps were used to fight fires from the mid-1800s to the early 1900s.

Modern protective clothing allows fire-fighters to walk through flames.

Some fire-fighting equipment

axe

sledge hammer

chain-saw

fire extinguisher

compressed air mask and cylinder

bolt cutters

rope

smoke extractor

flight simulator *noun*

A flight simulator is a machine which copies the actions of an **aircraft** in flight. Flight simulators stay on the ground. They are used to train pilots.

She learned how to land and take off in a flight simulator.

The pilot sits in a cockpit which has controls like those in a real aeroplane. A hydraulic system moves the platform to copy the movements of an aeroplane.

Three projectors produce a computer image on the screen which is three-dimensional. This means the image has depth, as well as height and width.

floppy disk *noun*
A floppy disk is a part of a **computer**. It is a magnetic disc inside a stiff, plastic envelope. A floppy disk is used to store information for the computer to work with.
He put the floppy disk into the disk drive of the computer.

flow chart *noun*
A flow chart is a kind of diagram. It shows the different stages in which a task must be carried out.
He used a flow chart to work out how to find the answer to the problem.

fluorescent lamp *noun*
A fluorescent lamp is a kind of light. It lights up when an **electric current** passes through gas in a sealed tube. The gas is a mixture of argon and mercury vapour. Most fluorescent lamps give a bright, white light.
The factory was brightly lit by fluorescent lamps.

flywheel *noun*
A flywheel is a part of some **engines**. It is a heavy wheel which is made to spin by the running engine. A flywheel stores **energy** to even out the power produced by the **pistons**.
They saw the traction engine's flywheel spinning round.

focal plane shutter *noun*
A focal plane shutter is a part of some **cameras**. It controls the length of time that the **film** is exposed to the light when a **photograph** is taken.
She set the focal plane shutter to expose the film for a fraction of a second.

food processor *noun*
A food processor is an **appliance**. It chops, mixes or minces food for use in cooking. A food processor has an **electric motor** and a large bowl.
She used her food processor to mix up the fruit for the pudding.

force *noun*
Force is a push or a pull. Forces make things move or change their shape. They are released by different kinds of **energy**.
Magnetic force made the iron filings cling to the magnet.

fork-lift truck *noun*
A fork-lift truck is a large machine. It is used to lift objects up, or put them down and move them from place to place. It has a double-pronged platform at the front, which can be raised and lowered by using **hydraulic** rams. The driver operates the controls from a cab, or walking behind.
There were several fork-lift trucks moving about the factory floor.

fork

hydraulic rams

fossil fuel *noun*
A fossil fuel is a solid, liquid or gas which was living matter millions of years ago. It is found under the ground. Fossil fuels are used to provide **energy**. Coal, oil and natural gas are fossil fuels.
Fossil fuels are dug or pumped from underground.

foundry *noun*
A foundry is a kind of factory where metal and glass objects are made. The metal or glass is heated to a very high temperature until it melts. It is then poured into moulds which give the objects their shape.
Cast iron pots and pans are made in a foundry.

four-colour printing   *noun*
Four-colour printing is a method of printing full-colour pictures by using four basic colours – red, blue, yellow and black. Pictures are broken down into tiny dots, each of which is one of the four basic colours. Then, when printed on a special four-colour press, the tiny dots can combine to form any colour that is desired.
Many newspapers are printed using the four-colour process.

four-stroke engine   *noun*
A four-stroke engine is a kind of **internal combustion engine**. The four strokes are movements of a **piston** inside the engine. The piston sucks a mixture of air and **fuel** in and **compresses** it. Then the piston moves down as the mixture of air and fuel burns and expands.
Most cars are powered by four-stroke engines.

four-wheel drive   *noun*
Four-wheel drive is a term which describes the way some vehicles are powered. Power from the **engine** is passed to all four wheels.
Four-wheel drive vehicles can easily be driven over rough or muddy ground.

fractional distillation   *noun*
Fractional distillation is a way of separating a mixture of liquids. The mixture is boiled, and the vapour rises inside a **fractionating column**. The vapour forms into different liquids at different levels of the column, as the temperature lowers.
Many different products are made from oil by fractional distillation.

fractionating column   *noun*
A fractionating column is part of an **oil refinery**. It is a tall tower that is hot at the bottom and cooler at the top. Trays at different levels collect products separated by **fractional distillation**.
Products are pumped away from the fractionating column to be stored.

freezer   *noun*
A freezer is an electrical **appliance** found in many homes. A freezer stores food at a low temperature. The food is frozen so that it stays fresh for a long time. A freezer works by pumping heat away from the air and food inside it.
We stored the ice-cream in the freezer.

friction   *noun*
Friction describes what happens when moving objects rub against each other. Friction makes them slow down and produces heat. **Lubricants**, such as **oil**, are used in **machines** to reduce the amount of friction between their moving parts.
Friction between the brake pads and the brake discs caused the car to slow down.

fridge ► **refrigerator**

frigate   *noun*
A frigate is a kind of **warship**. It has **missiles** and **guns** on deck and sometimes carries a **helicopter**.
They were shown over the frigate and saw how the guns were fired.

fuel   *noun*
Fuel is a substance which is burned to provide energy. The fuel for **internal combustion engines** is **petroleum** or **diesel fuel**. **Uranium** is a fuel which is used to **generate electricity** in **nuclear power stations**.
Coal and gas are kinds of fuel.

function   *noun*
1. A function is the purpose to which a **machine** or **device** is put.
The function of a refrigerator is to keep food cool.
2. A function is a process used in **calculation**. Addition and subtraction are functions. **Electronic calculators** have **keys** which are pressed to choose different functions.
We found the total by pressing the function key for addition.

funnel *noun*

1. A funnel is a part of some **engines**. It is a pipe from which the exhaust gases are pushed out, or expelled.
Steam puffed out of the ship's funnel.

2. A funnel is an instrument which is used for pouring liquids into small openings. It is wide at the top and narrow at the bottom.
He poured petrol into the car through a funnel.

furnace *noun*

A furnace is a machine for heating things. It burns **fuel** or uses **electricity** to produce great heat. Furnaces are used to heat water and melt metals.
He shovelled more coal into the furnace to make it hotter.

bricks

steel cover

waste material

molten iron

fuselage *noun*

A fuselage is the body of an **aircraft**. It contains the flight deck, the passenger compartments and the baggage hold.
The airliner has a long, thin fuselage.

G

galvanize *noun*

Galvanize describes a way of protecting iron and steel by giving them a coating of molten zinc. The zinc keeps air away from the iron or steel and stops it rusting.
Nails used for roofing are galvanized so that they will not rust.

gantry *noun*

A gantry is a kind of **crane**. It is built into the ceiling of a factory or warehouse. Chains hanging from the gantry can move objects around the factory floor.
They took care to avoid the hook hanging from the gantry in the warehouse.

gas *noun*

A gas is a substance. A gas always spreads out to fill its container. It is easy to compress a gas. Oxygen and carbon dioxide are two different kinds of gas. Some gases are used as **fuel** for machines.
Butane gas is a fuel used in camping stoves.

gas fire *noun*

A gas fire is a heating **appliance**. It burns natural or bottled gas which produces flames and heat. The gas comes out in small jets so that the fire can be lit safely.
It was a cold day, so they lit the gas fire.

gas laser *noun*

A gas laser is a **device** which uses a mixture of **gases**, such as neon and helium, to produce intense light energy. Gas lasers are used in laser light shows.
The stage was lit by coloured lights made by gas lasers.

gas turbine *noun*
A gas turbine is a machine which produces **energy**. It burns a mixture of **fuel** and **compressed air**. This produces hot gases which rush through a turbine as they expand. The turbine turns a **drive shaft** which is attached to it.
Jet aircraft are powered by gas turbine engines.

gasohol *noun*
Gasohol is a liquid **fuel**. It is a mixture of **petroleum** and alcohol. The alcohol is made from sugar cane or grain.
Gasohol is sold as a fuel for cars in some countries.

gasoline ► petrol

gastroscope *noun*
A gastroscope is an instrument used by doctors in hospitals. It is a hollow tube which is passed down through a person's mouth into their stomach. Using mirrors, doctors can study and photograph the inside of the stomach.
The doctor used a gastroscope to find out if the patient had a stomach ulcer.

gate *noun*
A gate is a kind of switch. It is part of a **computer**. A gate controls the flow of **electric current** through the computer's **integrated circuit**. This control makes the computer program work properly.
A computer contains thousands of gates in a very small space.

gear ► page 60

gearbox *noun*
A gearbox is a part of an **engine**. It contains shafts with a set of **gears** on each. The shafts can spin at different speeds so that the maximum power of the engine can be used.
The gearbox of a car is connected to the engine.

gear lever *noun*
A gear lever is a control found in an **engine**. It is used to change from one **gear** to another. This sends maximum power from the engine to the **drive shaft** of a machine.
Once the car was moving, she used the gear lever to change into second gear.

gear wheel ► gear

gearing *noun*
Gearing is the transfer of power from an **engine** to the **drive shaft** of a machine. Low gearing is used to start a machine moving. High gearing is used for great speed.
The racing car could reach such high speeds because it had high gearing.

generator *noun*
A generator is a machine for making **electricity**. It has a **shaft** which is turned by an **engine** or **turbine**. This movement makes **electric current** flow into wires which are connected to the generator.
There was no electricity because the generator at the power station broke down.
generate *verb*

carrying frame
starter engine
petrol engine
electric generator
fuel tank

glass *noun*
Glass is a hard, solid substance. It is made from sand and other materials. When melted, or molten, glass can be made into plates for windows, or into objects such as drinking glasses and test tubes.
We could not see out of the windows because the glass was dirty.

glider *noun*

A glider is a kind of aircraft which has no **engine**. To launch a glider, it is either towed by a powered aircraft or shot from the ground by a kind of catapult. Once it is launched, it is kept aloft by rising air currents.

When the towrope was released, the glider soared up into the sky.

glycerine *noun*

Glycerine is a sticky liquid which dissolves in water. It is used as a **lubricant** in machines for making cloth and food.

The ice-cream machine was lubricated by glycerine to avoid spoiling the ice-cream with oil.

gravure printing *noun*

Gravure printing is a kind of printing process. The type or picture to be printed is **etched** into a printing plate. When ink is wiped over the surface, some stays in the etched parts and is printed onto the paper.

The colour magazine was produced by gravure printing.

grinder *noun*

A grinder is a **machine tool** which is used to shape metal. **Gears** are made by grinding steel **discs** into shape using rough-surfaced materials called abrasives.

The mechanic made a new part for the machine by grinding a piece of metal.

handle

mill wheel

collecting tray

guitar ▸ electric guitar

gun *noun*

A gun is a **device** which fires objects from a tube. Guns can fire shot, shells or **bullets**. Special kinds of gun are used to shoot rivets into sheets of metal to join them together.

The race began when he fired the starting gun.

gunmetal *noun*

Gunmetal is a metal made from eight parts of **copper** to one part of **tin**. It is very strong. Gunmetal is used to make parts of machines which need strength but where steel cannot be used. It is no longer used to make guns.

Gunmetal is a kind of bronze.

gyrocompass *noun*

A gyrocompass is an instrument used in ships and aircraft to find the right direction to travel. It contains a **wheel** which spins freely on an **axle**. The axle always points in the same direction. It has a **dial** that is worked like a **compass**.

The pilot looked at the gyrocompass to make sure that he was flying due south.

gyroscope *noun*

A gyroscope is a wheel which is set to spin. Once it is moving, it is difficult to tilt. A **gyrocompass** contains a gyroscope.

Gyroscopes are used to keep ships steady in rough seas.

gyroscopic *adjective*

gear *noun*

A gear is a **wheel** with teeth called **cogs** around its edge. Its teeth fit, or mesh, with the teeth of other gears to make them turn. Gears use the **energy** produced by an **engine** to turn wheels or propellers. Gears can also change the direction of a force. *Top gear is used when a car is travelling at speed on a clear, level road.*

sprockets

gear lever mechanism

pedal

chain

chain-wheel

gear-changing mechanism

A derailleur gear on a bicycle has four toothed wheels, or sprockets, of different sizes. They are connected to the chain-wheel by a chain and turn the back wheel at different speeds, to suit the steepness of the road.

Worm gears change the direction of movement, and also speed and force. They have a shaft with a screw thread which meshes with a toothed wheel.

Bevel gears have two wheels which join, or mesh, together at an angle. This changes the direction of turning, or rotation. They may also change speed and force if necessary.

Rack and pinion gears change turning, or rotary, motion to to-and-fro, or reciprocating, motion. One wheel, called the pinion, meshes with a sliding, toothed rack.

H

hair-drier *noun*
A hair-drier is an electrical **appliance**. It contains a **fan**, an **electric motor** and a small **heater**. The fan blows warm air onto the hair of the person using the drier.
She used a hair-drier on her hair, which had got wet in the rain.

hair spring *noun*
A hair spring is part of a **watch**. It is a thin, metal wire **spring** which provides the power to move the hands of the watch.
His watch does not work because the hair spring has broken.

halogen lamp *noun*
A halogen lamp is a kind of electric **light bulb**. It gives out more light than an ordinary bulb. A halogen lamp contains iodine which allows the filament inside the bulb to be brighter and hotter.
The halogen lamp lit up the whole garden.

hammer *noun*
A hammer is a tool. It has two parts, the handle and the head. Some hammers are used to drive nails into surfaces. Others are used to beat metal into shape.
He used a hammer to drive a nail into the wall.

hand drill *noun*
A hand drill is a tool used to make holes in wood. It has a **ratchet** which is turned with a handle. The ratchet turns a metal bit or **drill** which bores into the wood.
The carpenter had a hand drill in his tool-kit.

hang glider *noun*
A hang glider is a kind of **aircraft**. Its wings are fixed to a light, metal frame. The pilot hangs underneath in a harness. Some hang gliders are fitted with small engines. These are called microlights.
Hang gliders are launched into the wind down a steep slope.

hard copy *noun*
Hard copy is information which is printed onto paper. It is produced by a **computer** or a **fax** machine.
She used a printer to make a hard copy of the file on the floppy disk.

hard disk *noun*
A hard disk stores information in some kinds of **computer**. This is done by using **electric signals** on a magnetic surface. Unlike a floppy disk, a hard disk cannot be removed from a computer. Hard disks can normally store more information than a floppy disc of the same size.
The hard disk spins at high speed inside the computer.

hardware *noun*
Hardware is all the working parts of a **computer**. The disk drive, the central processing unit, the input devices, such as the keyboard, and the output devices, such as the printer, are all hardware.
She looked at the instruction book to find out how to connect the computer's hardware.

harvesters *noun*

Harvesters are machines which gather farm crops when they are ripe. Harvesters are pulled by **tractors** or have their own engines.
The harvester dug up the sugar beet.

headphones *noun*

Headphones are appliances used to hear sounds without disturbing other people. They fit over each ear and are joined by a metal or plastic band which goes across the head. Headphones can be connected to a tape recorder or record player and work like a telephone **receiver**.
He listened to his new album on his headphones.

signal to amplifier

electromagnet   cone

heart-lung machine *noun*

A heart-lung machine is a **device** used in hospitals. It copies the action of the human heart and lungs and helps to keep a person alive during a serious illness or operation.
The hospital's operating theatre was equipped with a heart-lung machine.

heat exchanger *noun*

A heat exchanger is a **device** which moves heat from one place to another. **Air conditioners** often contain heat exchangers.
The office was kept cool by a heat exchanger.

heater *noun*

A heater is any **device** which warms things. Radiators, electric fires and coke boilers are all heaters.
He turned on the electric heater to warm up the room.

helical gear *noun*

A helical gear is a **gear wheel**. Its teeth are set at an angle to the shaft. When they are moving, helical gears make less noise than gears with straight teeth.
The car's gearbox was fitted with helical gears so it would run quietly.

helicopter *noun*

A helicopter is a kind of **aircraft**. It has rotor blades above the **fuselage** which support it in the air.
A helicopter can take off or land by moving straight up or down.

hi-fi *noun*

Hi-fi is short for high fidelity. High fidelity recordings of music sound almost exactly like the original performance.
He has bought some new hi-fi equipment for his records and tapes.

hinge *noun*

A hinge is a **device** which allows doors to open and close. It is made of metal. The two parts of the hinge are joined by a rod or hinge pin and move freely around it. Hinges can be found on doors, gates, covers or lids.
He forgot to close the door properly and it swung on its hinges.

hoist   *noun*
A hoist is a machine for lifting large objects, such as cars. Hoists are used in garages so that mechanics can work underneath cars. They are powered by an **electric motor**.
The mechanic raised the vehicle on a hoist so that he could inspect the chassis.

horn   *noun*
A horn is a **device** which makes a loud noise. Horns are used to give a warning. They are fitted to road vehicles, ships and sometimes to machines in factories. They may be powered by **electricity** or **compressed air**.
The ship sounded its horn in case it could not be seen in the thick fog.

horsepower   *noun*
Horsepower is a unit of measurement. It measures how fast work is done. One horsepower is equal to raising a load of 4,500 kilograms one metre in one minute. The abbreviation for horsepower is hp.
The car was powered by a 100 horsepower engine.

hot-air balloon   *noun*
A hot-air balloon is a kind of **aircraft**. It is made of nylon. The balloon is open at the bottom. A burner is used to fill it with hot air. The balloon rises into the air because the hot air inside it is lighter than the cold air outside. A basket is slung underneath the balloon to carry passengers and the burner.
He operated the burner and the hot-air balloon began to rise.

hovercraft   *noun*
A hovercraft is a vehicle which can be used over water, marshy ground or flat land. It is powered by a **gas turbine** or **petrol engine**. Fans make a cushion of air on which the hovercraft floats. There are **propellers** on deck to push the hovercraft forward.
A flexible curtain, called a skirt, keeps the cushion of air under a hovercraft as it travels along.

hub   *noun*
A hub is the centre of a **wheel**. The hub rotates round the **axle**.
The spokes of a bicycle wheel connect the hub to the wheel rim.

hydraulic   *adjective*
Hydraulic describes machines that are operated by the movement of liquids. Liquid under pressure is made to move a **piston** inside a cylinder. Because liquid cannot be compressed, great **force** can be released with little effort.
Most motor cars have hydraulic brakes.
hydraulics *noun*

hydraulic damper   *noun*
A hydraulic damper is a part of a vehicle. It smooths out the effect of bumps in the road. A hydraulic damper is connected between the wheels and the body of the vehicle.
When a wheel goes over a bump, the hydraulic damper takes in, or absorbs, the shock.

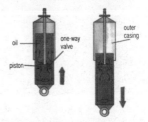

hydraulic fluid   *noun*
Hydraulic fluid is usually a type of **oil**. It is used in hydraulic machines, such as a **fork-lift truck**. Modern hydraulic engines use fluids that do not freeze at low temperatures. These fluids include oil, certain silicones and some gases.
He topped up the hydraulic fluid container to make sure that the brakes worked properly.

hydraulic gearboxes   *plural noun*
Hydraulic gearboxes are parts of some cars.
They use **hydraulic fluid** to send power
from the **engine** to the **drive shaft**.
A car with hydraulic gears does not need a
clutch.

hydraulic jack   *noun*
A hydraulic jack is a **device** which uses the
pressure of a liquid forced through an
opening to lift an object. It has a platform
which is placed under the object to be lifted.
A **lever** works a **piston** which makes the
platform rise.
The mechanic used a hydraulic jack to
change the car's wheel.

platform

piston

oil reservoir

high pressure oil

hydraulic press   *noun*
A hydraulic press is a machine which
shapes sheets of metal. It uses **hydraulic**
power to press the sheets down with great
force onto a shaped surface. A hydraulic
jack and hydraulic brakes use the same
system as a hydraulic press.
Car bodies are shaped with a hydraulic
press.

hydraulic ram   *noun*
A hydraulic ram is a machine used in
building work. It uses **hydraulic** power to
operate a heavy weight which rams earth
into a solid mass.
The road-builders used a hydraulic ram to
make a firm foundation for the road.

hydraulic robot   *noun*
A hydraulic robot is a machine which is used
to perform tasks in factories. **Hydraulics**
provide the power to operate tools
automatically. Hydraulic robots are
controlled by **computers**.
Hydraulic robots fitted parts to the car bodies
on the factory assembly line.

hydraulic system   *noun*
A hydraulic system is a way of transmitting
hydraulic power over a long distance. It is
made up of a number of hydraulic cylinders
joined by pipes. A large pump sends
hydraulic fluid flowing through the system.
The factory's hydraulic system provided
hydraulic power for every department.

hydro-electric power   *noun*
Hydro-electric power is **electricity** which is
generated by the power of flowing water.
The water spins a **turbine** which drives an
electric **generator**.
Hydro-electric power stations need a good
supply of fast-flowing water.

hydro-electric turbine   *noun*
A hydro-electric turbine is part of a hydro-
electric power station. It has blades like fan
blades which are turned by the flow of water.
The turbine's **drive shaft** powers an electric
generator.
Water flowed from sluices in the dam into
the hydro-electric turbine.

generator

turbine
blades

hydrofoil ► page 66

hydrofoil *noun*

1. A hydrofoil is a device shaped like an aircraft wing. It is used on or under water. Because of its shape, water flows more quickly over the top surface than the bottom. *Some liners are fitted with hydrofoils to keep them steady in rough seas.*

2. A hydrofoil is also a kind of **ship** which travels just above the surface of the water on hydrofoils.
A hydrofoil can reach high speeds because water resistance does not slow it down.

A hydrofoil is like a wing that goes through water. This hydrofoil is used by the United States Navy and carries guided missiles.

Hydrofoils can travel twice as fast as other kinds of ship. They are often used as passenger ferries.

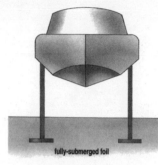

fully-submerged foil

In fully-submerged hydrofoils, the foils stay completely under water. These hydrofoils can be used in rough seas, but need stabilizers to keep them steady.

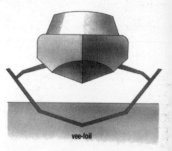

vee-foil

Part of the vee-foil appears above the surface of the water as the vessel moves forward. This type of hydrofoil was easier to develop than submerged ones, but can only be used in calm, coastal waters.

shallow draft foil

The shallow draft foil is fully submerged, but can keep steady without stabilizers.

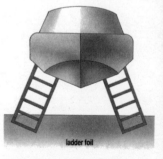

ladder foil

The ladder foil was used in an early hydrofoil built in 1918. It set a world water speed record of 114 kilometres per hour. The record remained unbroken until 1963.

hydrogen bomb   *noun*
A hydrogen bomb is a **nuclear weapon**.
It explodes with great force when hydrogen
atoms are joined together in the process of
nuclear fusion. Hydrogen bombs have never
been used in wartime.
The explosion of a hydrogen bomb produces
great heat and releases enormous
destructive energy.

hydrophone   *noun*
A hydrophone is a **device** for hearing
sounds under water. It receives sound
waves and converts them into **electric**
signals. These signals can be seen on a
meter or played through a loudspeaker.
Fishermen use hydrophones to help them
find shoals of fish.

hydroplane   *noun*
A hydroplane is part of a **submarine**.
Hydroplanes are fitted in pairs at the front
and back of the hull. They look like short
fins. They can be tilted to raise or lower the
depth of the submarine.
Hydroplanes help a submarine to dive and
surface.

hydroplane   *verb*
Hydroplane describes the action of an object
when it slides along on a film of water. An
ice-skater hydroplanes on the film of water
on top of the ice.
The accident was caused when the car
hydroplaned on a patch of water in the road.

hypodermic syringe   *noun*
A hypodermic syringe is a **device** which
injects substances under the skin of a
person or animal. It is fitted with a hollow,
pointed needle. Doctors sometimes use a
hypodermic syringe to inject a patient with
medicine.
My doctor used a hypodermic syringe to give
me a vaccine to protect me from influenza.

ignition system ► page 69

incandescent lamp   *noun*
An incandescent lamp is a **light bulb** which
contains a thin wire, or filament. **Electricity**
passing through the wire makes it glow.
Thomas Alva Edison was the inventor of the
incandescent lamp.

inclined plane   *noun*
An inclined plane is a **simple machine**. It is
a sloping surface. It is easier to push an
object up an inclined plane than to lift it.
A screw has an inclined plane running round
it from top to bottom.

induction motor ► **linear induction**
motor

inertia   *noun*
Inertia explains why all objects need a push
to make them move. If an object has a large
mass, it will also have a large inertia. **Force**
works against the inertia of an object and
changes its speed or direction.
A cannonball has a larger inertia than a
tennis ball.

information technology ► page 70

inkjet printer ► **bubblejet printer**

input   *noun*
An input is information which is loaded into a
computer. It is put there by devices such as
keyboards, **joysticks** and **floppy disks**.
He used a keyboard to type an input into the
computer.

ignition system   *noun*

An ignition system is part of some **internal combustion engines**. It uses electricity to make a spark which causes the mixture of fuel and air in the **cylinders** to explode.
The ignition system sends bursts of electricity to the sparking plugs.

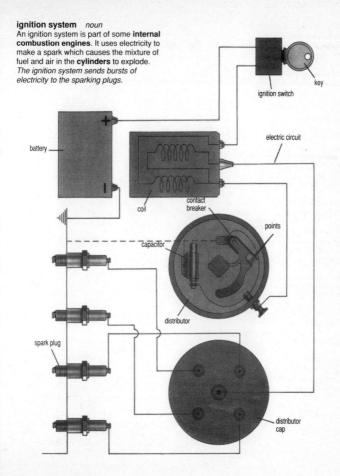

key

ignition switch

electric circuit

battery

coil

contact breaker

points

capacitor

distributor

spark plug

distributor cap

information technology   *noun*
Information technology is the study of the
use of information. **Computers**, **fax**,
television and **radio** are all forms of
information technology.
Information technology uses data in the form
of electric signals.

A fax machine sends and receives printed messages over
telephone wires.

A computer can solve problems, and store and supply
information, at great speed.

Viewdata is a type of information system used by travel agents and some other businesses. People using viewdata can key in data as well as receive it. Viewdata is connected by telephone lines to a central computer.

A radio can be tuned to different wavelengths to receive many different programmes. It receives radio signals from a transmitter and changes them into sound.

A television may receive its programmes in three different ways. Signals may come from a land-based transmitter through the atmosphere. They may travel along fibre optic cables underground, or via a satellite circling the Earth.

71

internal combustion engine noun

An internal combustion engine is an **engine** which burns fuel inside. **Petrol** and **diesel engines**, and **gas turbines**, are internal combustion engines.

You cannot see the working parts of internal combustion engines because they are hidden.

A diesel internal combustion engine runs on diesel fuel. It does not have spark plugs to ignite the fuel like a petrol engine. Instead, the very high pressure inside the cylinder raises the temperature of the mixture of air and fuel until it explodes.

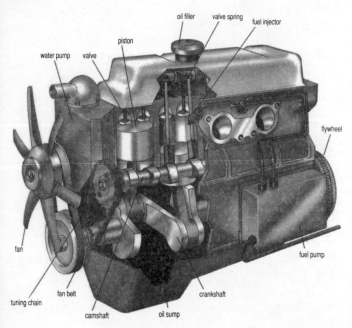

oil filler valve spring fuel injector

piston

water pump valve

flywheel

fan

fuel pump

tuning chain

fan belt

camshaft oil sump crankshaft

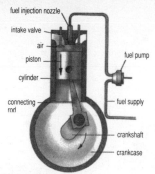

fuel injection nozzle
intake valve
air
piston
cylinder
connecting rod
fuel pump
fuel supply
crankshaft
crankcase

1. Intake stroke
The piston moves down and draws air into the cylinder.

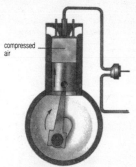

compressed air

2. Compression stroke
The piston moves up and squeezes, or compresses, the air. Air temperature rises to about 480°C.

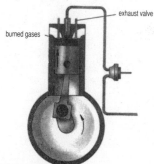

burned gases
exhaust valve

4. Exhaust stroke
Piston moves up and forces exhaust gases out of the cylinder.

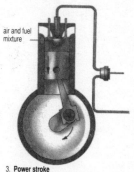

air and fuel mixture

3. Power stroke
Fuel injected into cylinder where it mixes with hot air and explodes. Gases produced by explosion push piston down.

73

insulator   *noun*

An insulator is a substance or a device which stops the flow of heat or electricity. The plastic covering on **electric cables** is an insulator. **Asbestos** is an insulator against heat.

The insulators on the pylons prevented electricity from reaching the ground.
insulate   *verb*

integrated circuit   *noun*

An integrated circuit is a part of **electronic** equipment. It is a **silicon chip** which has **electric circuits** engraved on it. An integrated circuit is also called a chip or a microchip.

When a computer is working, thousands of signals flow through its integrated circuits.

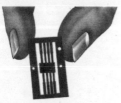

interface   *noun*

An interface is part of a computer. It is an **electric cable** with a plug at each end. It connects parts of the computer together.
They could not connect up the computer because they did not have the right interface.

internal combustion engine   ▶ page 72

inventor   *noun*

An inventor is someone who uses his imagination to create a new machine or other device. An inventor may try to market his own invention or he may sell it to a large company.
Alexander Graham Bell was the inventor of the telephone system in 1875.

ionizer   ▶ air ionizer

iron   *noun*

1. Iron is a dark grey, **ferrous** metal. Cast iron is brittle and breaks easily. Iron is used to make steel for use in machines. Magnets attract iron.
When iron is left outside, it reacts with water vapour from the air which makes it rust.
2. An iron is an **appliance** for pressing items such as clothes and sheets. **Electricity** heats a smooth plate which is passed over the fabric. Some irons have a water container and send out steam as they move.
Her dress was creased, so she pressed it with an iron.

iron lung   *noun*

An iron lung is a machine used in hospitals. It is used to help sick patients to breathe. An iron lung does the work of the chest muscles that the patient cannot use.
The iron lung forced air in and out of the patient's lungs.

IT   ▶ information technology

J

jack *noun*

A jack is a machine for lifting objects from below. A car jack lifts a wheel off the ground so that the wheel can be changed. Small jacks can be made to work by turning a handle. Larger jacks use **hydraulic** power.
She had a puncture, so she took out the jack to change the wheel.

jet aeroplane *noun*

A jet aeroplane is an **aircraft** fitted with jet engines. Most fighter aircraft and large **airliners** are jet aeroplanes.
The jet aeroplane made a sudden noise as it swooped overhead.

jet engine *noun*

A jet engine is an **engine** which sucks in air and pushes out a jet of hot gases. The gases come out with such force that they push the engine forwards. The gases are produced by a **gas turbine**.
They could see the heat haze caused by the jet engines as the aircraft took off.

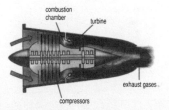

combustion chamber
turbine
exhaust gases
compressors

jet pack *noun*

A jet pack is a **device** which allows an astronaut to move about in space. It is strapped to the astronaut's back. The astronaut can make it send out a jet of **compressed air** which pushes him in any direction he wants.
The astronaut used his jet pack to move about outside the spacecraft.

joystick *noun*

1. A joystick, or control column, is the name for one of the controls of an **aircraft**. The pilot pushes it forwards to dive, backwards to climb and left or right to turn.
After take-off, the pilot pulled on the joystick to climb to his planned height.
2. A joystick is one of the **input** devices which can be used with a **computer**. It is a handle which is connected by cable to the computer. A joystick is used to control the picture on the visual display unit.
Joysticks are often used to play computer games.

jump jet *noun*

A jump jet is a kind of **aircraft**. It can take off or land vertically. The jet thrust from its **jet engine** can be made to point downwards. Some jump jets can also fly sideways or backwards. Jump jets are sometimes called vertical take-off and landing aircraft, or VTOLs.
A jump jet does not need a runway to land on.

K

kerosene *noun*

Kerosene is a liquid **fuel** made from **oil**. It is used in **jet engines**. Another name for kerosene is paraffin.
The jet aeroplane's fuel tanks were filled with kerosene.

key *noun*

1. A key is a button which is found on a **keyboard** or **keypad**. When it is pressed, it sends instructions or **data** to a **computer** or **electronic calculator**.
She pressed the addition key on her calculator to find the total.
2. A key is a small rod or strip of metal used to open a **lock**. It has a pattern cut into it which fits the inside of the lock.
You will not be able to open the lock unless you have the right key.

key   pin   cylinder

keyboard *noun*

A keyboard is part of a **computer**. It has rows of **keys**. Some keys have letters or numbers on them. Others carry out certain **functions**. A keyboard is a computer **input**.
A keyboard is used to feed data into a computer.

keypad *noun*

A keypad is a small **keyboard**. It has no more than 20 **keys**. An **electronic calculator** has a keypad which is used to feed in numbers and **functions**.
The plus sign on a keypad marks the key which is used for addition.

kilobyte *noun*

A kilobyte is a unit of measurement. It is used to describe the size of the **memory** in a computer or the amount of **data** that can be stored on a **floppy disk** or a **hard disk**. A kilobyte is the same as 1,000 **bytes**. It is sometimes shortened to KB.
The floppy disk could hold up to 720 kilobytes of information.

kinetic energy *noun*

Kinetic energy is **energy** which objects have when they are moving. It is the energy of movement. If an object is heavy and moves quickly, it has a large amount of kinetic energy. Machines which use **fuel** turn chemical energy into kinetic energy. Wind and flowing water also have kinetic energy.
Everything that is moving has kinetic energy.

kite *noun*

A kite is a small **device** which flies. It has **aerofoils** which are supported by the flow of air over them. A kite is controlled from the ground by a person holding a string.
We went to the beach and flew our kites.

laminate *noun*

A laminate is a material made from a number of layers of substances which are stuck together. Laminates made from wood and plastics are often used for office and kitchen furniture.
The kitchen worktop was made from a laminate of chipboard and plastic.
laminate *verb*

landing gear *noun*

The landing gear, or undercarriage, is the equipment which an **aircraft** uses when it takes off or lands. It is usually a set of **wheels** underneath or wings. Most aircraft pull in, or retract, their landing gear into the fuselage when in flight.
The pilot lowered the aeroplane's landing gear as he approached the airport.

laser *noun*

A laser is a **device** which uses light energy to perform tasks. It produces a narrow beam of very bright, powerful light. A laser can be used to cut metal. Lasers are also used by doctors to carry out operations, and in **fibre optics**.
Laser light can be directed to where it is needed by using mirrors.

laser printer *noun*

A laser printer is an output device for some **computers**. **Electronic signals** from the central processing unit are changed into pulses of laser light. This makes images on a drum. Ink powder sticks to the images and is transferred onto paper.
She used a laser printer to copy her drawing.

laser scalpel *noun*

A laser scalpel is an instrument used in hospitals to destroy diseased body tissue. Laser scalpels prevent the loss of blood during operations as they do not cut blood vessels.
The surgeon used a laser scalpel to carry out an operation on the boy's eye.

lathe *noun*

A lathe is a **machine tool**. It is used to cut, shape or polish wood or metal. An object is held tightly in the lathe and turned round, or rotated. Special turning tools are used to carry out work on the object. Small lathes can be powered by a foot pedal called a treadle. Larger lathes have an **electric motor**. Many parts of car engines are made with a lathe
He shaped the chair leg on a lathe.

launcher *noun*

A launcher is a kind of **rocket**. It is used to send objects into space. A launcher burns **chemicals** to provide the power for the first stage of the object's journey.
Clouds of burning gas poured out of the launcher as the spacecraft lifted off.

lawn mower *noun*

A lawn mower is an **appliance** for cutting grass. Some mowers have rows of blades formed into a hollow cylinder across the front of the machine. Others have disc blades fitted beneath the machine.
Some rotary lawn mowers have long, flat blades that spin flat when they cut the grass.

lawn sprinkler *noun*

A lawn sprinkler is a **device** for sprinkling water evenly over a lawn. It is connected to a water supply. The force of the water pushes round a nozzle inside the sprinkler. This makes sure that each part of the lawn round the sprinkler is watered.
There had been no rain for days, so they watered the grass with a lawn sprinkler.

leaf spring   *noun*
A leaf spring is part of a **vehicle**. It is made up of strips of special steel. The ends of the spring are fixed to the **chassis** of the vehicle. It is fixed to an **axle** at the centre. The leaf spring absorbs shocks from the surface on which the vehicle is travelling.
The cart was fitted with leaf springs which made our ride more comfortable.

lens ► concave lens and convex lens

letterpress printing   *noun*
Letterpress printing is a printing process. The surface of the characters or images to be printed is raised. A film of ink is spread over the surface and then pressed onto paper.
Letterpress printing was used to produce the poster for the meeting.

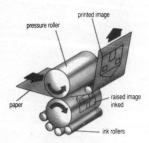

pressure roller

printed image

paper

raised image inked

ink rollers

lever ► page 80

lift   *noun*
A lift is a machine which carries objects or people from one level to another. It is powered by **hydraulics** or by an **electric motor**. Many offices and stores have lifts. A lift is sometimes called an elevator.
We rode to the sixth floor of the building in a lift to avoid taking the stairs.
lift   *verb*

light bulb   *noun*
A light bulb is a **device** which uses **electricity** to produce light. It is made of glass. The bulb contains a thin wire called a filament, which is usually made of tungsten. The bulb is filled with a gas which stops the filament from becoming brittle.
When electricity flows through a light bulb filament, it glows brightly.

light meter   *noun*
A light meter is a **device** which measures the amount of light. It is used by a photographer to set the camera so that it takes a bright picture.
She used a light meter to check the camera setting needed to take the picture.

light pen   *noun*
A light pen is a **device** used in some shops and libraries. It is passed over a **bar code**. A light pen changes light signals from the bar code into **electric signals**. These are sent along an **electric cable** to a computer.
The shop assistant ran her light pen over the bar code on the label of the can.

lightning conductor   *noun*
A lightning conductor is a length of thick wire. One end is fixed to the top of a building and the other is buried in the ground.
A lightning conductor carries lightning safely into the ground and prevents a building being damaged if it is struck.

linear induction motor *noun*
A linear induction motor is an **electric motor**. The motor makes an electromagnetic field. Moveable parts of a machine are either pushed away or pulled forwards by the motor. As the pushing and pulling effects work in turn, the moveable parts can travel along a track. If the linear induction motors are large enough to support the weight of a rail carriage, they could power a transport system.
Sliding doors are often operated by linear induction motors.

liquid crystal display *noun*
A liquid crystal display is a **device** which lights up to show letters, numbers or images. It looks like a very small **screen**. The display changes when different **electric signals** are fed into it. The abbreviation for liquid crystal display is LCD. LCDs are found in **electronic calculators** and in some digital clocks and watches.
The liquid crystal display on my watch showed that it was time to leave for school.

lithographic printing *noun*
Lithographic printing is a printing process. The letters or images to be printed are marked on a printing plate with a greasy substance. The rest of the plate is made wet. When ink is rolled onto the plate, it sticks only to the greasy parts. The ink is then transferred to paper. Offset lithography is a kind of lithographic printing.
Many books are produced by lithographic printing.

load *noun*
A load is a weight or **force** that is supported by a structure or any part of a structure. It is also a weight that another force pushes or pulls. Beams, bridges and pillars support loads. **Levers**, pulleys and other machines move loads. Forces produced by machines act in the opposite direction to the load.
The bulldozer moved the load of earth from the middle to the edge of the road.

lock *noun*
A lock is a **device** which keeps objects secure. Some locks will open only when a key of the right shape is inserted. Others are **combination locks** and can only be opened with a **code** number.
She turned the key in the lock to open her travel bag.
lock *verb*

long-wave radio *noun*
Long-wave radio is a method of transmitting and receiving signals by radio over long distances.
We listened to a programme from abroad by long-wave radio.

loom *noun*
A loom is a **weaving machine** for making cloth. It weaves threads, or yarn, above and below each other so that they stay tightly together. Looms are either hand-driven or power-driven.
Power looms are usually found in factories and are run by electricity, water or steam.

loudspeaker *noun*
A loudspeaker is a part of a radio, television or record player. It changes **electric signals** into sounds. The sound comes out of the front of the loudspeaker.
He turned up the volume of the loudspeaker so that he could hear the news.

79

lever *noun*

1. A lever is a **simple machine**. It is a bar which rests at one point on a firm surface. This point is called the fulcrum. Effort is applied at one end of the lever. This effort lifts a weight, or **load**, at the other end.
Seesaws and wheelbarrows are kinds of lever.

2. A lever is a device used to operate machines. It is a kind of switch. Moving the lever makes the machine behave in a certain way.
The car driver used the gear lever to change gear.

Second-class levers

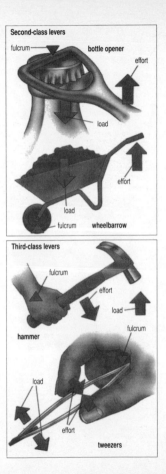

bottle opener

wheelbarrow

First-class levers

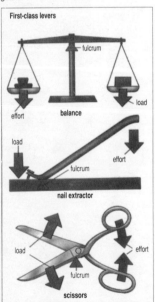

balance

nail extractor

scissors

Third-class levers

hammer

tweezers

Multiple levers

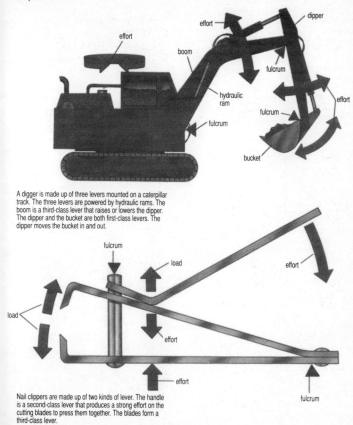

A digger is made up of three levers mounted on a caterpillar track. The three levers are powered by hydraulic rams. The boom is a third-class lever that raises or lowers the dipper. The dipper and the bucket are both first-class levers. The dipper moves the bucket in and out.

Nail clippers are made up of two kinds of lever. The handle is a second-class lever that produces a strong effort on the cutting blades to press them together. The blades form a third-class lever.

81

lubricant *noun*
A lubricant is a slippery liquid. Lubricants make the moving parts of **machines** slide smoothly against each other and reduce the amount of **friction**. **Oil** is used as a lubricant in car **engines** and many other machines.
The car was not running smoothly because there was not enough lubricant in the engine.
lubricate *verb*

machine *noun*
A machine is any **device** which does work. It changes the direction or strength of a **force** applied to it. Screws, levers, wheels, wedges, inclined planes and pulleys are all **simple machines**. These simple machines go together to make up more complicated machines, such as engines and motors. Machine also describes any device which has moving parts.
A sewing machine is useful for making clothes.

machine language *noun*
Machine language is a set of instructions that a computer can use without having to translate it.
Machine language is formed in binary code.

machine tool *noun*
A machine tool is a tool which is powered by a **machine**. **Lathes** and **electric drills** are examples of machine tools.
In the factory, machine tools were used to cut and shape the parts of the engine.

maglev train *noun*
A maglev train is a **train** which runs on a special track. It has a **linear induction motor**. Magnetic forces hold the train a few millimetres above the track. When **electromagnets** in the train are switched on and off, the train moves forward. Maglev is short for magnetic levitation.
A maglev train carried passengers from the airport to the main-line railway station.

magnetic levitation ► **maglev train**

magnetic compass   *noun*
A magnetic compass is an instrument for finding the way. It has a **dial** containing a needle which always points to magnetic north.
Although it was foggy, they were able to find their way home with a magnetic compass.

magnetic tape   *noun*
Magnetic tape is a long ribbon of plastic coated with magnetic particles. **Electric signals** change the pattern of the particles on the tape. Magnetic tape is used in **tape recorders**, **video cassette recorders** and some **computers**.
A video cassette contains magnetic tape inside a plastic case.

magnifying glass   *noun*
A magnifying glass is a device which makes objects appear larger. It is made up of a **convex lens** in a metal or plastic case. It may have a handle to hold it with.
The print was so small that he had to use a magnifying glass to read it.

mainframe computer   *noun*
A mainframe computer is the largest and most powerful kind of **computer**. It can fill a whole room. Mainframe computers are found in the offices of large companies. They can process very large amounts of **data** and do several jobs at once.
A telephone company uses a mainframe computer to work out how much customers have to pay.

manned manoeuvring unit   *noun*
A manned manoeuvring unit, or MMU for short, is a **device** used in space exploration. It has its own air supply for the people using it. Jets of compressed air blown out of a jet pack allow a MMU to move around.
The astronauts used a manned manoeuvring unit to explore the surface of the Moon.

measuring machines   *noun*
Measuring machines are **devices** used to calculate measurements. **Scales**, **meters** and **micrometers** are different kinds of measuring machine.
A weighbridge is a measuring machine used to weigh loaded vehicles.

mechanical   *adjective*
Mechanical describes a machine. Engines, lifts, cranes and bicycles are all mechanical. They all contain moving parts which are connected together.
A mechanic is someone who has learned mechanical skills.

mechanical energy   *noun*
Mechanical energy is **energy** which is produced by machines. An **engine** changes chemical energy in a **fuel** into mechanical energy. Mechanical energy does work by moving things. It means the same as **kinetic energy**.
A bicycle turns human energy into mechanical energy.

mechanical mole *noun*

A mechanical mole is a machine for boring tunnels through rock. It works like a giant **drill**. A mechanical mole has sharp teeth which turn, or rotate, at high speed and tear the rock away.
The mechanical mole dug a tunnel under the mountain for a new road.

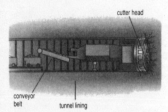

cutter head

conveyor belt

tunnel lining

medium-wave radio *noun*

Medium-wave radio is a method of transmitting and receiving signals by radio. Medium-wave radio can be received several hundred kilometres from the **transmitter**.
Some small radios can receive programmes only on medium-wave radio.

megabyte *noun*

A megabyte is a unit of measurement. It is used to measure the amount of **data** or information on a **floppy disk** or in the **memory** of a computer. One megabyte is the same as 1,000,000 bytes or 1,000 kilobytes.
The abbreviation for megabytes is MB.

memory *noun*

A memory is a part of a **computer**. There are two kinds of memory. One is **random access memory** and the other is **read-only memory**. **Data** and **programs** are stored in these memories. The size of the memory is measured in **kilobytes** or **megabytes**.
A read-only memory is part of a computer's central processing unit.

metal detector *noun*

A metal detector is a **device** for discovering metal hidden underground. It sends out **electric signals**. If they strike metal, they send a sound signal back to the user.
Metal detectors are often used by treasure hunters who are looking for old coins, jewellery and other valuable objects.

meter *noun*

A meter is a **measuring machine**. Water meters measure the flow of water. Electricity meters measure the flow of electricity. Meters can be either **analogue** or **digital**.
She looked at the meter to see how much electricity the family had used.

microchip ► integrated circuit

microcomputer *noun*

A microcomputer is the smallest kind of **computer**. It is sometimes called a personal computer. Microcomputers are used in many homes, schools and small offices.
She used a microcomputer to do her maths homework.

micrometer *noun*

A micrometer is a **measuring machine**. It measures very small distances. The object to be measured is held between two jaws. A **scale** shows the distance between the jaws, which is the measurement of the object.
The engineer measured the thickness of the metal with a micrometer.

microphone   *noun*
A microphone is a **device** used to change sound waves into **electrical signals**. Microphones are used in radio and in sound recording.
There is a small microphone in the mouthpiece of a telephone.

microprocessor   *noun*
A microprocessor is an **integrated circuit**. It is a part of a **computer**. It controls the **data** and **programs** which the computer uses. Microprocessors are also found in digital watches, electronic calculators, and some appliances such as automatic washing machines.
The invention of the microprocessor allowed very small computers to be made.

microscope   *noun*
A microscope is an instrument which can make very small objects seem much larger. An ordinary microscope contains **lenses**. An **electron microscope** uses an **electron gun** to magnify objects.
He used a microscope to study a grain of sand.

microwave oven   *noun*
A microwave oven is a cooking **appliance**. Microwaves are very short **radio waves**. When they strike food, particles of the food vibrate against each other. This produces heat by **friction** and cooks the food.
A meal can be prepared very quickly using a microwave oven.

milking machine   *noun*
A milking machine is a **dairy machine** used for milking cows. It pumps the milk away from the cow's udders to a storage container. The suction pump is driven by **electricity**.
Milking machines are found in a farm's milking parlour.

mincer   *noun*
A mincer is an **appliance** used in cooking. It cuts food into small pieces. A mincer can be worked by hand or powered by an **electric motor**.
She put the meat through the mincer and then put it in the pie.

mirror   *noun*
A mirror is a **device** which reflects light. It is usually made of glass coated on one side with a silver substance. A mirror presents an image of objects in front of it.
Before he went out he looked at himself in the mirror.

missile   *noun*
1. A missile is anything that is pushed forward by force. **Bullets** and artillery shells are missiles.
The crowd threw stones and other missiles at the robbers.
2. A missile is a **vehicle** which carries an explosive warhead. It can be fired in the air or in space. Missiles are powered by **rocket motors** or by **jet engines**.
The bomber was shot down by a ground-to-air missile.

model   *noun*
1. A model is a small copy of something larger. Engineers often build models to help them find out how real machines will behave.
The engineers tested a model of the new airliner in a wind-tunnel.
2. A model is a version of a machine that existed before in a slightly different form.
He exchanged his old car for this year's model.

multi-stage rocket *noun*

A multi-stage rocket is a **vehicle** used to put
objects into space. It has **rocket motors** in
each stage. Each motor takes the vehicle
part of the way.

*A multi-stage rocket was used to put the
satellite into space.*

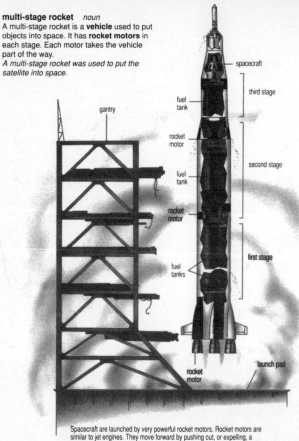

gantry

spacecraft

third stage

fuel
tank

rocket
motor

second stage

fuel
tank

rocket
motor

first stage

fuel
tanks

rocket
motor

launch pad

Spacecraft are launched by very powerful rocket motors. Rocket motors are
similar to jet engines. They move forward by pushing out, or expelling, a
powerful stream of burning gases.

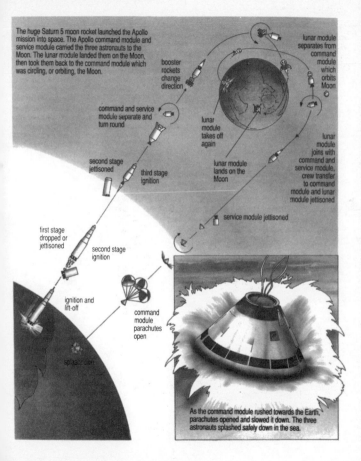

The huge Saturn 5 moon rocket launched the Apollo mission into space. The Apollo command module and service module carried the three astronauts to the Moon. The lunar module landed them on the Moon, then took them back to the command module which was circling, or orbiting, the Moon.

lunar module separates from command module which orbits Moon

booster rockets change direction

command and service module separate and turn round

lunar module takes off again

second stage jettisoned

third stage ignition

lunar module lands on the Moon

lunar module joins with command and service module, crew transfer to command module and lunar module jettisoned

service module jettisoned

first stage dropped or jettisoned

second stage ignition

ignition and lift-off

command module parachutes open

As the command module rushed towards the Earth, parachutes opened and slowed it down. The three astronauts splashed safely down in the sea.

87

modem *noun*
A modem is a **device** which is used with some **computers**. It connects the computer to a telephone line.
Computers with modems can send information to each other over telephone lines.

motion picture *noun*
A motion picture is a **film** which is shown in a cinema. It is shown using a **movie projector**. Motion pictures are sometimes called movies.
He went to see a motion picture about Christopher Columbus.

motor *noun*
A motor is a kind of machine. Motors change chemical, electrical or other kinds of **energy** into **mechanical energy**. This mechanical energy is used to do work. Electric motors and engines are different kinds of motor.
The toy car was powered by a clockwork motor.

motor car ► **automobile**

motor cycle *noun*
A motor cycle is a two-wheeled road vehicle. It has an **internal combustion engine** which burns **petrol**. Large motor cycles can carry a passenger who sits behind the driver.
He gave his brother a ride on his new motor cycle.

mouse *noun*
A mouse is a **device** which is used with some **computers**. It is a small box with buttons on top and a ball underneath. When the mouse is moved over a surface, the ball rolls and a marker appears on the **visual display unit**. Pressing the buttons on the mouse gives instructions to the computer.
A mouse tells a computer to carry out different functions.

mouthpiece *noun*
A mouthpiece is part of a **telephone**. It is the part that a person speaks into. A mouthpiece contains a small **microphone** which sends **electric signals** down the telephone line.
She picked up the telephone and spoke into the mouthpiece.

movie camera *noun*
A movie camera is a kind of **camera** which is used to make **motion pictures**. It contains an **electric motor** which winds the film through the camera and takes thousands of photographs one after the other.
The movie camera began to roll and the actors started playing their parts.

movie projector *noun*
A movie projector is a machine for showing **motion pictures**. It unwinds a film in front of a bright light. The pictures on the film are projected through **lenses** onto a screen.
He loaded a new film into the movie projector.

multi-stage rocket ► page 86

N

nail clipper *noun*
A nail clipper is a **device** for cutting finger and toe nails. It clips the ends off with a sharp blade, and works with a **lever** mechanism.
He trimmed his finger nails with a nail clipper.

nail extractor *noun*
A nail extractor is a **device** for removing nails from wood or other materials. A claw **hammer** has a nail extractor at one end of the head. The claw is placed under the head of the nail and the handle of the hammer is used as a **lever** to pull the nail out.
Before he started work, he had to remove all the old nails with a nail extractor.

natural gas *noun*
Natural gas is a **fossil fuel**. It is a mixture of a number of different **gases** which burn when they are ignited. Natural gas is tapped or pumped from wells. Many homes in towns and cities can be connected to a natural gas supply.
Natural gas heated the water and cooked the food.

network *noun*
A network describes two or more **computers** which are linked up so that they work together. Computers in a network can share information and **data**.
All the schools in the city were linked by a computer network.

neutron bomb *noun*
A neutron bomb is a powerful **nuclear weapon**. It can kill soldiers on a battlefield but do little harm to nearby civilians and buildings.
A neutron bomb can be dropped from an aircraft or used as the warhead of a missile.

non-return valve *noun*
A non-return valve is a **device** which allows gas or liquid to pass through in only one direction.
The air in the tyre cannot escape because it is pumped in through a non-return valve.

nuclear *adjective*
Nuclear describes the breaking apart or joining together of atoms. The breaking apart of atoms is called nuclear fission. Joining atoms together is called nuclear fusion. Both these processes cause the release of nuclear **energy**.
Modern submarines are nuclear powered.

nuclear power station *noun*
A nuclear power station generates **electricity**. Heat from a **nuclear reactor** boils water to produce steam. The steam drives the shaft of a **generator**.
Nuclear power stations are often near the sea, which carries away waste water produced by the power stations.

nuclear reactor *noun*
A nuclear reactor is a device which uses **nuclear** fuel to release **energy**. The reactor in a **nuclear power station** produces heat which boils water to make steam.
A nuclear reactor is surrounded by a thick, concrete wall.

nuclear weapon   *noun*

A nuclear weapon is a bomb or missile which contains a **nuclear** warhead. It can be dropped from an **aircraft**, fired from a **gun** or fitted with a **rocket motor**.
Many people would like to see a worldwide ban on the making of nuclear weapons.

numerically-controlled machine tool
noun

A numerically-controlled machine tool is a **machine tool** which is connected to a **computer**. The computer sends instructions to the machine tool, which then performs tasks **automatically**. NMT is short for numerically-controlled machine tools.
Most of the work in the factory was done by numerically-controlled machine tools.

nut   *noun*

A nut is a fastening device. It is a piece of metal with four or six sides and a hole in the middle. Inside the hole is a spiral groove called a thread. This fits with the thread on a **bolt**. Nuts and bolts are used to fasten things together.
He used a spanner to tighten the nut around the bolt.

nutcracker   *noun*

A nutcracker is a device for breaking open the shells of nuts. It is a kind of **lever**. The fulcrum of this lever is at one end, with the **load** in the middle. The nutcracker's jaws crush the shell when the handles are squeezed together.
The nuts were so hard that it was difficult to open them even with a nutcracker.

nylon   *noun*

Nylon is a kind of **plastic**. It is made from **chemicals**. Nylon fibres can be spun into cloth or ropes. Pieces of hard nylon are often used for small **machine** parts.
The lining of his anorak was made of nylon.

O

offset lithography   *noun*
Offset lithography describes a kind of **lithographic printing**. The image on the lithographic plate is transferred to a roller. Then the roller is inked and pressed onto the paper.
Most newspapers are printed by offset lithography.

oil   *noun*
An oil is a kind of fatty or greasy liquid that does not mix or dissolve in water, but will dissolve in alcohol. Many oils are used as **lubricants**. When used as a lubricant, a film of oil is spread over the moving parts of a **machine** to reduce **friction**. Most lubricating oil is made from **petroleum** but other kinds of oil, such as castor oil, are sometimes used as lubricants.
He oiled his bicycle so that it would be easy to pedal.

oil lamp   *noun*
An oil lamp is a kind of lamp which uses **oil** as fuel. The oil is stored at the bottom of the lamp and soaks up a wick to the burner, where it is lit, or ignited.
There was no electricity in the house, so they found their way upstairs with an oil lamp.

oil pump   *noun*
An oil pump is part of many machines. It pumps **oil** to places in the machine where **lubricant** is needed. Lubricants reduce **friction** and take away heat.
The oil pump in a motor car pumps oil around the moving parts of the engine.

oil refinery   *noun*
An oil refinery is a place where **petroleum** is processed into different substances. The petroleum is heated in a **furnace**. A **fractionating column** then separates the petroleum into different liquids and gases.
Products made at an oil refinery have many uses.

oil rig ► page 92

oil tanker   *noun*
An oil tanker is a kind of **ship**. It is built to carry large amounts of **oil** or oil products. Oil tankers call at special ports called **oil terminals**.
The oil tanker was carrying many thousands of tonnes of kerosene.

oil terminal   *noun*
An oil terminal is a port where **oil tankers** load or unload their cargoes. Oil terminals are equipped with **pumps**, storage tanks and **pipelines**.
The oil tanker is due to sail from the oil terminal tomorrow.

ophthalmoscope   *noun*
An ophthalmoscope is an instrument used to inspect a person's eyes for disease or damage. It shines a narrow beam of light through the iris into the eyeball.
The optician asked the girl to open her eyes while he looked at them through an ophthalmoscope.

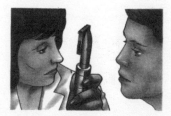

oil rig *noun*

An oil rig is a structure which is found at an oil well on land or at sea. It is a tower which contains a **drill**. The drill bores into the ground or sea-bed below the rig. Exploration rigs search for new supplies of oil. Production rigs pump oil to the surface.
Work on an oil rig at sea is hard and often dangerous.

living quarters

crane for unloading supplies from boats

drill

helicopter landing pad

anchor chain to sea-bed

air tanks to keep rig upright

a semi-submersible drilling rig

1. Tug boats tow the base of a production platform out to sea on its side.

2. The boats turn the base over and it is set upon the sea-bed.

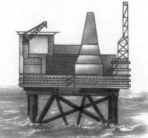

3. Decks are placed on the production platform and a crane lifts a block of buildings onto the decks.

4. The production rig is ready for work.

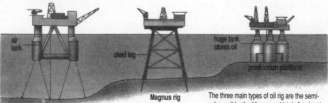

air tank

steel leg

huge tank stores oil

production platform

semi-submersible rig

Magnus rig

The three main types of oil rig are the semi-submersible, the Magnus, which is fixed to the sea-bed by huge steel legs, and the production platform.

93

optical fibre *noun*

An optical fibre is a thin, hollow thread made from glass. Optical fibres are bundled together to make optical cables. Messages in the form of light signals are sent along optical fibres by using laser light.
Cables made up of optical fibres can carry more messages than copper wire cables.

optical instruments *noun*

Optical instruments are instruments which make use of light energy. They usually have **lenses** to direct the flow of light. **Telescopes** and **binoculars** are optical instruments.
Optical instruments are very carefully made to make sure they are accurate.

output *noun*

Output describes what is produced by a machine or other device. The output of a **computer** can be seen on a **screen** or printed on paper. The output from a factory is the goods it makes.
The output from a record player is the sound that comes through the loudspeaker or earphones.

overshot waterwheel *noun*

An overshot waterwheel is a kind of **engine** driven by water power. The water supply is piped so that it pours out above the waterwheel and drops on to it, making it turn round, or rotate. The rotation is used to drive machinery.
Power from an overshot waterwheel was once used to grind corn into flour.

P

pacemaker *noun*

A pacemaker is a **device** which is fitted into the body of a person with heart disease. It is powered by a tiny **battery**. This gives out **electric signals** which help the person's heart to beat regularly.
Her grandfather went into hospital to be fitted with a pacemaker.

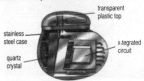

transparent plastic top

stainless steel case

integrated circuit

quartz crystal

padlock *noun*

A padlock is a kind of **lock**. It is used to secure objects which are not fitted with locks of their own. It has a curved bar which can be slipped through a chain or other strong fixture. Most padlocks have **keys**, but some are **combination locks**.
He secured his bicycle with a padlock so that it would not be stolen.

parachute *noun*

A parachute is a device which slows down objects that are falling through air. It has a canopy made of silk or nylon cloth. Ropes connect the canopy to a harness. When it is not being used, a parachute is folded into a small package. When it opens, the canopy resists, or pushes against, the air flowing past it.
The aircraft crashed out of control but the pilot landed safely by parachute.

paraffin *noun*
Paraffin is another name for **kerosene**. It is a **fuel** made from **petroleum**.
She filled the lamp with paraffin and lit it.

parking meter *noun*
A parking meter is a **device** which shows how long a vehicle has been parked in a particular space. It is operated by a coin. The coin starts a **clockwork motor** which drives a needle, showing how much time has gone by.
He found a place to park and put some money in the parking meter.

pedal-power plane *noun*
A pedal-power plane is an **aircraft** which is powered by human energy. It has pedals like a bicycle. Movement of the pedals makes a **propeller** turn and pull the plane through the air.
Pedal-power planes are made and flown for fun.

pedometer *noun*
A pedometer is a **device** which is carried by someone walking. The mechanism inside a pedometer records each step the walker takes and so works out the distance travelled.
His pedometer showed that he had walked nearly 10 kilometres.

pendulum clock ► page 96

pendulum seismograph *noun*
A pendulum seismograph is a type of **seismograph**. It is a **device** for recording the strength of earthquakes. It has a pendulum attached to a pen which marks paper fixed to a drum. Earthquake waves make the drum move, but the pendulum stays still.
The pendulum seismograph showed that the earthquake had been a severe one.

percolator *noun*
A percolator is a **device** for making coffee. Boiling water rises up a tube in the centre of the percolator and drains down through a filter containing ground coffee.
After the meal, they had fresh coffee made with a percolator.

periscope *noun*
A periscope is a **device** which allows people to see over or round objects. It uses mirrors to reflect rays of light from the object to our eyes. Periscopes in **submarines** allow the crew to see above the surface of the sea.
He used a periscope to see over the wall into the garden.

personal computer ► **microcomputer**

personal stereo *noun*
A personal stereo is a small **cassette tape recorder** which can be carried in the pocket or in a small case. It has **earphones** so that tapes can be heard in private. Some personal stereos also have a **radio.** Some record sound as well as play it back.
She listened to some music on her personal stereo.

petrol *noun*
Petrol is the **fuel** used in a **petrol engine**. It is a **fossil fuel** which comes from **petroleum**. Petrol is sometimes called gasoline.
They called at the filling station to fill the car's tank with petrol.

pendulum clock   *noun*
A pendulum clock is a **clock** with a
pendulum which helps it keep accurate time.
A pendulum is a long rod with a weight on
one end. The other end is connected to a
clockwork motor. The pendulum swings to
and fro and the length of its swing can be
adjusted to make the clock faster or slower.
Grandfather clocks are pendulum clocks.

anchor

drive wheel

cog wheel

minute
hand

hour
hand

pendulum

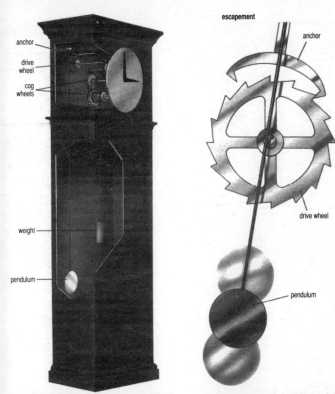

escapement

anchor

drive wheel

cog wheels

anchor

drive wheel

weight

pendulum

pendulum

A grandfather clock has a pendulum to make sure it keeps good time. As it swings, the pendulum rocks the anchor which controls the turning of the drive wheel.

The escapement makes the hands tick forwards. As it rocks to one side, the anchor catches in the cogs of the drive wheel and stops it moving. As the anchor rocks to the other side, the drive wheel is released for a short time. The weight on the drive wheel falls, turning the drive wheel and hands.

petrol engine *noun*
A petrol engine is a kind of **internal combustion engine**. It burns a mixture of **petrol** and air in a cylinder. This releases energy which moves a **piston**.
Her new motor cycle had a petrol engine.

petrol pump *noun*
A petrol pump is a device for supplying road vehicles with **petrol** or **diesel fuel**. It pumps fuel from a storage tank into the vehicle's fuel tank.
People can serve themselves with petrol at a self-service petrol pump.

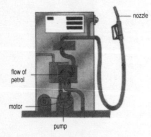

nozzle

flow of petrol

motor

pump

petroleum *noun*
Petroleum is a dark, oily liquid which is found beneath the surface of the Earth. It contains many different products which are separated at an **oil refinery**. Another name for petroleum is crude oil.
Petroleum is taken out of the ground by drilling down to it and pumping it up.

photo booth *noun*
A photo booth is a cubicle which contains an automatic **camera**. A person operates the camera by putting coins in a slot. It uses an **electronic flash** to take photographs.
She needed a new passport photograph, so she went to a photo booth.

photocopier ► page 100

photograph *noun*
A photograph is an image recorded on **film** by a camera. The film is sensitive to light. A photograph may be in colour or in black and white.
On the shelf there was a photograph taken when he was two years old.

phototransistor *noun*
A phototransistor is a kind of **sensor**. It is an electrical device which is sensitive to light. Light falling on a phototransistor can be used to switch an **appliance** on or off. Phototransistors are used to operate automatic doors and in some **burglar alarms**.
When the car cut off the light falling on the phototransistor, the garage doors opened.

piano *noun*
A piano is a large musical instrument. It contains strings which make musical notes when they are struck by felt hammers. The player presses keys on the piano's keyboard to move the hammers.
She sat at the piano and played a tune.

pig iron *noun*
Pig iron is a grey metal. It is made in a **blast furnace**. While it is still liquid, it is poured into moulds to set into blocks which are called pigs. Most pig iron is used to make **steel**.
Pig iron is hard but brittle and breaks easily.

pile-driver   *noun*
A pile-driver is a machine which drives metal or concrete posts into the ground. It has a very heavy **hammer** which is raised by a crane and then allowed to drop.
The builders used a pile-driver to make the foundations of the new office block.

pipeline   *noun*
A pipeline is a long pipe which is usually laid underground. It is used to carry liquids or gases over long distances. Pipelines are usually made of **steel**, **plastic** or concrete.
The pipeline carried petroleum from the oil well to the oil refinery.

piston   *noun*
A piston is a part of a machine. It moves backwards and forwards inside a **cylinder**. When vapour in the cylinder expands, it forces the piston down, producing **mechanical energy**. Pistons are found in **internal combustion engines**, **pumps** and **hydraulic** systems.
The pistons in a car engine make the crankshaft rotate.

plane   *noun*
1. A plane is a hand tool. It is used to smooth and shape wood. It is made up of a box-like frame with a handle at each end. The flat, metal base has a slit with a sharp blade sticking through.
As the plane moved across the wood, the blade shaved off a thin sliver of material.
2. A plane is a flat surface. An **inclined plane** is a plane which is raised at one end. It is a kind of **simple machine**.
The top of a table is a plane.

planetary gears   *plural noun*
Planetary gears are **gear wheels** which are arranged in a special way. The 'planet' wheels move round a central 'sun' wheel. They take their name from the way the planets move round the Sun.
Planetary gears are found in cars which have automatic gearboxes.

plastic   *noun*
Plastic is an artificial material. It can be moulded into different shapes. Plastic is made by mixing **chemicals**. **Nylon** is one type of plastic.
The kitchen table had a top made of plastic.
plastic   *adjective*

platform scale   *noun*
A platform scale is a **weighing machine**. The object to be weighed is placed on a platform. The weight is shown in grams and kilograms on a kind of **meter**.
Bathroom scales are one kind of platform scale.

pliers   *plural noun*
Pliers are small tools. They grasp objects between two claws. Pliers are often used to hold hot metal while it is being worked on. They are a simple **lever**.
The blacksmith held the horseshoe with a pair of pliers.

plough   *noun*
A plough is a machine which digs land ready for seeds to be sown. It has a blade which digs into the soil and turns it over. Some ploughs have one or two rows of blades. Ploughs are usually pulled by tractors.
There were deep furrows in the field where the plough had been.
plough   *verb*

photocopier *noun*

A photocopier is an appliance which makes copies of books or sheets of paper. It makes the copies by using static **electricity** or **chemicals**. A photocopier produces copies which look exactly the same as the original.
She used a photocopier to make several copies of her poem.

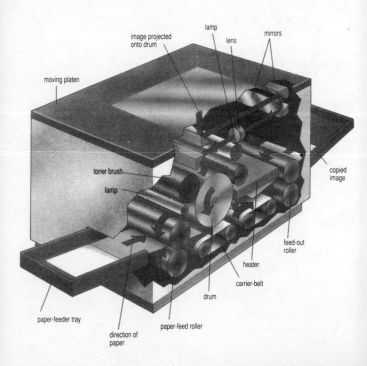

moving platen

image projected onto drum

lamp

lens

mirrors

toner brush

lamp

copied image

feed-out roller

heater

carrier-belt

paper-feeder tray

direction of paper

paper-feed roller

drum

The photocopying process

1. Electricity flows through the metal plate or cylinder and charges it.

2. A lens focuses the image onto the plate.

3. Toning powder is brushed over the plate and sticks to the image.

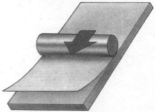

4. A piece of paper is pressed onto the plate.

5. The toning powder on the image sticks to the paper.

6. Heated rollers make the image permanent.

pneumatic *adjective*
Pneumatic describes a device that is
powered by **compressed air**. An **air
hammer** is a pneumatic device.
*Pneumatic machines are often used to build
and mend roads.*

pneumatic drill *noun*
A pneumatic drill is a tool which is used for
making holes in the ground. It is driven by
compressed air.
*The workman used a pneumatic drill to
make a hole in the pavement for the new
road sign.*

pneumatic machine *noun*
A pneumatic machine is a machine which is
driven by **compressed air**. The compressed
air is supplied by another machine which is
called a **compressor**.
*The car repairer used a pneumatic polisher
to finish the car's new paint.*

points *plural noun*
1. Points are part of a railway track. They
switch **trains** from one set of rails to another.
Railway points are sometimes called
switches.
*At the points, the train turned on to the main
line.*
2. Points are part of the **ignition system** of
an internal combustion engine. They control
the flow of electricity to the **sparking plugs**.
Many new cars are fitted with an electronic
kind of ignition system which does not need
points.
*The car is not running well because the
points are dirty.*

post mill *noun*
A post mill is a kind of **windmill**. It has a
wooden mill house with sails attached to a
shaft. The shaft turns, or rotates, as the wind
drives the sails round. A post mill, including
the mill house, can be turned to face into the
wind.
*The village miller used to grind the farmers'
wheat in his post mill.*

potential energy *noun*
Potential energy is stored **energy**. Nuclear
energy and chemical energy are kinds of
potential energy. When an object is lifted
above the ground, it stores potential energy.
This energy becomes **kinetic energy** when
the object falls back to the ground.
*Potential energy was stored in the drawn
bowstring.*

potter's wheel *noun*
A potter's wheel is a machine for making
round, **cylindrical** objects out of clay. A ball
of clay is placed on the wheel. As the wheel
rotates, the potter shapes it with his hands.
*We learned how to make a jug on the
potter's wheel.*

power *noun*
Power describes how much work is done in
a certain length of time. The power of an
engine is the greatest amount of work it can
do to drive a **machine**. The power of a **light
bulb** is the amount of light it gives out and
how much **electricity** it uses. In the metric
system power is measured in watts. But
because a watt is a very small unit it is
better to measure power in kilowatts, which
is units of 1,000 watts. The power of a
car is measured in horse power which is
.746 kilowatts.
*His new motor cycle has twice as much
power as her scooter.*

power boat *noun*
A power boat is a **boat** with a powerful **engine**. It can accelerate quickly and travel through the water at high speed. The engine is mounted at the rear of the boat. Different kinds of power boats are used for racing in competitions around the world.
The power boat flashed past with a roar.

power drill *noun*
A power drill is a **drill** driven by an **electric motor**. It is used to make small, round holes in hard surfaces.
He used a power drill to make a hole in the wall.

power station *noun*
A power station is a place where **electricity** is made. In large power stations, fuel is burned to boil water and make steam. The steam spins a **turbine** which drives a **generator**.
A train carried coal to the power station for use in its boilers.

power take-off *noun*
Power take-off is a method of powering a farm machine. The **transmission** of a **tractor** has a shaft which sticks out from the rear axle. This is connected to the machine, so that a system of **gears** can **transmit** power from the tractor engine to the machine.
The farmer baled the straw with a baler driven by a power take-off.

pressure gauge *noun*
A pressure gauge is an instrument which measures the force of a gas or liquid. One kind of pressure gauge is used to test the pressure of air inside the **tyres** of road **vehicles**. The pressure is shown on a **scale** or a **meter**.
She used a pressure gauge to check whether her bicycle tyres had enough air in them.

print head *noun*
A print head is a part of a **printer**. It is the part which makes marks on the paper. The print head of a **daisy wheel printer** is a wheel with a number or letter on each spoke.
He cleaned the print head of the bubblejet printer because the holes were clogged and it was not printing clearly.

printer *noun*
A printer is a part of a **computer** or **word processor**. It prints the **output** from the computer or word processor on paper. The main kinds of printer are **daisy wheel**, **dot matrix**, **bubblejet** and **laser**.
Some printers can produce drawings or diagrams in different colours.

printing press ► page 104

processing unit ► **central processing unit**

processor ► **microprocessor**

product *noun*
A product is something which has been made. It is usually something that is made up of smaller parts. A product may be food or clothing, a **device** or an **appliance**. Most products are made in factories. Some products are put together, or assembled piece by piece on an **assembly line** by machines. Others are assembled by hand.
The plastics factory made plastics into many different products.

printing press *noun*

A printing press is a machine which is used to print on paper. Some presses print on paper cut into sheets. Others print on reels of paper. **Letterpress** presses and **offset lithography** presses are two kinds of printing press.

They saw the first copies of the newspaper to come off the printing press.

In offset lithography, a flat plate is treated, or etched, so that only the areas to be printed attract a greasy ink.

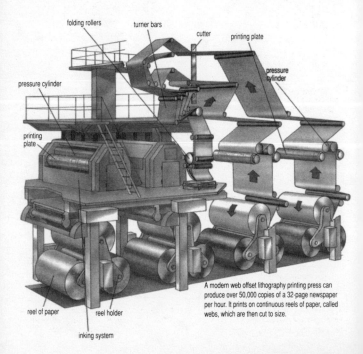

A modern web offset lithography printing press can produce over 50,000 copies of a 32-page newspaper per hour. It prints on continuous reels of paper, called webs, which are then cut to size.

folding rollers

turner bars

cutter

printing plate

pressure cylinder

pressure cylinder

printing plate

reel of paper

reel holder

inking system

Methods of printing

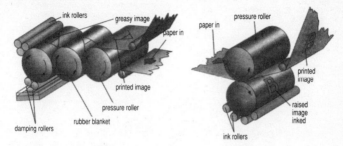

1. Offset lithography uses a flat plate which is treated to receive ink only on the areas to be printed. The inked image is transferred onto a rubber blanket which presses it onto the paper.

2. In letterpress printing, the image is a raised area on the plate. Only this raised area receives ink.

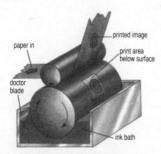

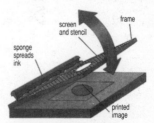

3. In gravure printing, the image is cut into the plate. The whole surface is inked. A doctor blade scrapes ink off the raised part, leaving only the image filled with ink.

4. In silk-screen printing, a stencil is laid on top of a screen made from very fine net. Ink is forced through the screen onto the paper and the stencil forms the image.

program *noun*

A program is a set of instructions which is loaded into a **computer**. It tells the computer how to perform different tasks. Programs are stored on **floppy disks**, **hard disks** or **magnetic tape**.
He used a floppy disk to load a new program into his computer.

projector *noun*

A projector is a device which throws an image through **lenses** onto a screen. The image is thrown by a bright light bulb. **Slide projectors** and **movie projectors** are two kinds of projector.
He put a reel of film in the projector and the movie show started.

focus knob · light bulb · lens · slide · lens

propeller *noun*

A propeller is a part of a **ship** and of some **aeroplanes**. It has two or more curved blades fixed to a shaft. The shaft is turned by an engine. As the propeller blades rotate, a **force** pushes or pulls the ship or aeroplane forwards.
The propellers of a ship cannot usually be seen because they are under water.

pulley *noun*

A pulley is a **simple machine**. It is a wheel with a groove around its outside edge. A rope or cable fits into this groove. Pulling on the rope or cable allows a weight on the other end to be lifted. Heavier loads can be lifted by using more than one pulley wheel on the same rope.
The mechanic lifted the engine out of the car by using a pulley.

pump *noun*

A pump is a device for moving liquids or gases from one place to another. The pump in a central heating system moves hot water through the pipes. **Centrifugal pumps** and **reciprocating pumps** are two kinds of pump.
She used a pump to fill her bicycle tyres with air.

pump *verb*

Q

R

quantum mechanics *noun*

Quantum mechanics describes the way some kinds of **energy** behave. These kinds of energy are made up of small bursts or waves of energy. Each burst is called a quantum. Light is one of the kinds of energy that behaves in this way.
The theory of quantum mechanics explains why light waves can be changed into small electric currents.

quartz clock *noun*

A quartz clock is a kind of **clock** which contains a crystal of a mineral called quartz. An **electric current** makes the quartz move backwards and forwards very quickly, or vibrate. The vibrations drive a small motor.
Quartz clocks keep very accurate time.

racing car *noun*

A racing car is a kind of **automobile**. It has a low, **streamlined** body and a very powerful engine. Racing cars are fitted with wide wheels to help them stay on the racing track.
The mechanic quickly changed the wheels and tyres on the racing car.

rack and pinion gears *plural noun*

Rack and pinion gears are gears which are used in the **steering system** of many cars. The pinion is a toothed **gear wheel** at the end of the steering column. It joins, or meshes, with the rack, which is a long, toothed rod. When the steering wheel is turned, rack and pinion gears change the turning, or rotary, movement into a push and pull movement.
Rack and pinion gears are connected to the front wheels of a car.

radar speed trap *noun*

A radar speed trap is a **device** for checking the speed of passing vehicles. It measures speed by using radar and displays it on a small screen.
The driver was travelling too fast in his car and the police caught him in a radar speed trap.

radar   *noun*
Radar is a way of finding the position of
objects. A radar set sends out **radio waves**.
These are bounced back, or reflected, by
certain objects and show up on the screen of
the radar set. Radar is used by **ships** and
aircraft to check their positions.
*The screen of the radar set showed that the
aeroplane was 20 kilometres from the
airport.*

radiator   *noun*
A radiator is an **appliance** which gives out
heat. In a central heating system, radiators
are supplied with hot water from a boiler.
The heat spreads out, or radiates, through a
room. Some radiators are filled with **oil**
which is heated by **electricity**.
*As soon as we reached home, we turned on
the radiators to warm the house.*

radio   *noun*
1. Radio is a means of electronic
communication. It makes use of **radio
waves** to send and receive signals.
The captain used his radio to call for help.
2. A radio is an electronic device which
receives radio signals and converts them
into sounds.
*She switched on her radio to hear the latest
news.*

radio dish   *noun*
A radio dish is a kind of **aerial**. It is shaped
like a shallow bowl. A radio dish collects
radio signals and passes them to a **radio
receiver**.
*The airport control tower had a radio dish
fixed to its outside wall.*

radio-pager   *noun*
A radio-pager is a small **radio receiver**.
People who are away from their place of
work sometimes carry a radio-pager. It
makes a bleeping sound when it receives a
radio signal from the caller.
*When the radio-pager bleeped, the doctor
knew she must telephone the hospital.*

radio receiver   *noun*
A radio receiver is an **appliance** for
receiving radio signals. It picks up the
signals from the **transmitter** and changes
them into sounds.
*He listened to the concert on his radio
receiver.*

radio telescope   *noun*
A radio telescope is a large instrument which
is used to study objects in space. It receives
radio signals from stars and other objects.
One kind of radio telescope receives signals
with a large **radio dish**.
*The dish on the radio telescope was moved
to make the signal clearer.*

radio transmitter   *noun*
A radio transmitter is an **electronic device**.
It sends out radio signals through an **aerial**.
These signals can be received by **radio
receivers** a long way away.
*The engineer switched on the radio
transmitter to start broadcasting at the
beginning of the day.*

radio wave   *noun*
A radio wave is a kind of **energy** which
moves through air and space. It can be
made to carry messages by adding **electric
signals** to it. These signals are sent out by
radio transmitters and can be heard on radio
receivers.
*Radio waves travel at a speed of 300,000
kilometres per second.*

raft *noun*

A raft is a simple **boat** with a flat bottom. Some rafts are just a platform with no sides. Others have sides. A raft can have a sail or be pushed along by oars or a pole.
They crossed the river on a raft they had built out of wood.

rally car *noun*

A rally car is an **automobile** which takes part in tests called rallies. It is an ordinary automobile fitted with special equipment. Rally driving is a popular sport. The driver must complete a set journey in a set time.
He spent many days preparing his rally car for the journey across Africa.

RAM ► **random access memory**

ramp *noun*

A ramp is an inclined plane which usually connects two different levels.
Ramps can be used to help people enter vehicles or buildings where steps cannot be used.

random access memory *noun*

A random access memory is part of a **computer**. It is made up of **integrated circuits**. The random access memory stores programs and data while work is being done on a computer. RAM is short for random access memory.
Information can be passed to the random access memory by using an input device.

ratchet *noun*

A ratchet is a kind of **gear** found in some tools and machines. It is a wheel or rod with teeth on its edge. The end of a **lever** joins, or meshes, with the teeth and allows the ratchet to move in only one direction.
He used a ratchet screwdriver to save time putting up the shelf.

raw material *noun*

Raw material is a natural substance used to make things. Sheep's wool is the raw material used by **spinning machines** to make wool yarn. Iron ore is the raw material used to make **steel**. Factories turn raw material into **products**.
Petroleum is the raw material from which petrochemicals and fuels are made.

reactor ► **nuclear reactor**

read-only memory *noun*

A read-only memory is part of a computer. It is made up of **integrated circuits**. A read-only memory contains instructions which tell the computer how to do its work.
Nothing can be added to a computer's read-only memory.

rear-wheel drive *noun*

Rear-wheel drive describes a vehicle in which the engine is connected to the rear wheels. Many motor cars have rear-wheel drive.
The car surged forward as the power of the six-cylinder engine was sent to the rear-wheel drive.

receiver *noun*
1. A receiver is a device for receiving **electronic signals** and changing them into sounds or pictures. **Radios**, **televisions** and parts of **radar sets** are receivers.
He listened to music on his radio receiver.
2. A receiver is the part of a telephone that is held to the ear. It receives **electric signals** down the telephone line and changes them into sounds.
He put the receiver to his ear to hear what his brother was saying.
receive *verb*

reciprocating pump *noun*
A reciprocating pump is a kind of **pump** which moves a liquid or a gas by using a **piston**. When the piston moves in one direction, it allows the liquid or gas to enter the cylinder. A bicycle pump is a reciprocating pump.
When the piston moves in the opposite direction, it pumps the liquid or gas out of the cylinder.

record player *noun*
A record player is an **appliance** which changes vibrations into **electric signals** and changes the signals into sounds. The sounds come out of a **loudspeaker**.
A record player contains a motor which spins records. It also has a pick-up which collects the electric signals.
Record players play records made of vinyl.

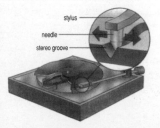

stylus

needle

stereo groove

refine *verb*
Refine describes how something is made purer. In an oil refinery, pure products are refined from crude oil. During refining, mixtures are separated and impure substances are removed.
White sugar is refined from sugar cane or beet so that it is completely pure.
refinery *noun*

reflecting telescope *noun*
A reflecting telescope is an **optical instrument** for studying the night sky. Objects in the sky are reflected in one or more **mirrors**, and then viewed through a **lens**.
He used a reflecting telescope to look at the planet Mars.

refractor telescope *noun*
A refractor telescope is an **optical instrument** for studying the night sky. Objects in the sky are viewed through two or more **lenses**. Refractor telescopes do not contain mirrors.
The boy could see many interesting things in the night sky with his refractor telescope.

refrigerator *noun*
A refrigerator is an **appliance** for keeping things cool. It contains a **pump** which circulates a **coolant** along pipes. Heat is transferred from inside the refrigerator to the coolant. Then the heat is given off into the room outside.
She looked in the refrigerator for a cold drink.
refrigerate *verb*

relay *noun*
A relay is a kind of switch which is used in many electrical devices. A small **electric current** flows through a device called an **electromagnet**. This makes an electric contact which switches an **electric circuit** on or off.
A relay can be used to switch an appliance on or off from a distance.

remote control unit *noun*

A remote control unit is a **device** which controls a machine or an **electric circuit** from a distance. Many remote control units use **radio waves** to send signals to a **receiver** inside the machine or circuit. Others may use a **phototransistor**.
He guided the model aeroplane with a remote control unit.

reprocessing *noun*

1. Reprocessing is the refining of impure substances into pure ones. **Chemicals** which have been mixed can sometimes be reprocessed to separate the different substances they contain.
Used nuclear fuel can be changed into pure plutonium by reprocessing.
2. Reprocessing describes how material which has been used once can be used again. Reprocessing can turn old jars and bottles from a bottle bank into new glass objects.
Old newspapers can be cleaned and turned into fresh, white paper by reprocessing.
reprocess *verb*

rescue machine *noun*

A rescue machine is a machine which is used to save trapped or injured people. **Helicopters** are often used as rescue machines.
Fire-fighters often use rescue machines to free people from blazing buildings.

resonator *noun*

A resonator is a **device** which makes sounds louder. It receives the vibrations of sound waves and makes them larger.
The paper, plastic or metal cone of a loudspeaker is a resonator.

rev counter ► **revolution counter**

revolution counter *noun*

A revolution counter is a **device** which counts the number of revolutions made by a part of an engine, such as a crankshaft. It shows the speed at which the engine is working. Some cars are fitted with a revolution counter.
A revolution counter on a tape recorder shows how many times the spool of tape has turned.

rivet *noun*

A rivet is a **device** for fastening two pieces of metal together. It is fixed in place with a hammer or a rivet gun. It does the job of a **nut** and **bolt**.
He fixed the number-plate to his car with rivets.

robot *noun*

A robot is a kind of machine which can do work without human help. Robots can do work that is too dangerous or boring for people to do. They are used in car factories to put together car bodies and paint them.
Some robots are designed to work under water.

rocket *noun*

A rocket is a **device** which is powered by a gas that it shoots out at high pressure. The gas is produced by the burning of fuel. The fuel used in firework rockets is gunpowder. Space rockets use mixtures of solids, liquids or gases.

Powerful rockets sent the spacecraft into orbit.

rocket motor *noun*

A rocket motor is an **engine** which works by burning fuel and pushing out, or expelling, gases at high pressure. **Spacecraft** are powered by rocket motors. Rocket motors contain **pumps** and other devices to control the burning of the fuel.

Rocket motors are the most powerful types of engine ever built.

rod thermostat *noun*

A rod thermostat is a **device** which controls the temperature of a liquid. It is fitted inside a **boiler**. A rod thermostat can be set to switch off the heat when the liquid reaches a certain temperature. It contains a switch which is sensitive to heat.

She set the thermostat on the boiler so that the bath water would not be too hot.

roll-on roll-off ferry *noun*

A roll-on roll-off ferry is a kind of **ship**. It has a ramp at one or both ends. The ramp is lowered when the ferry is in port. Vehicles can be driven on and off, which saves time in loading and unloading. RORO is short for roll-on roll-off ferry.

Many short sea crossings are made by roll-on roll-off ferry.

roller *noun*

A roller describes an object that rolls. A roller may be made of stone, metal, wood or plastic. It can be used for pressing, crushing or smoothing. Heavy rollers may be used for making or repairing roads or smoothing down grass on tennis courts.

Many lawnmowers have rollers attached.

roller blind *noun*

A roller blind is a kind of curtain or door. When the blind is up, it is stored round a roller. A roller blind can be pulled down all the way or it can be held in any position by a **ratchet**. Garages and workshops often have doors that are roller blinds made of strips of metal joined together.

She pulled down the roller blind to keep the sunlight off the furniture.

roller coaster *noun*

A roller coaster is a kind of ride found at a fairground. It has vehicles which travel along a track at high speed. The track goes up and down and round bends to make the ride more exciting.

She enjoyed the ride on the roller coaster, but she was screaming all the time.

ROM ► read-only memory

RORO ► roll-on roll-off ferry

rotary *adjective*

Rotary describes the circular action of part of a machine. A rotary lawn mover has a blade which moves or rotates in a circle, flat to the ground. Rotary blades can be found on helicopters. They rotate fast enough to allow the helicopter to lift off the ground. The sails on windmills also have a rotary action.

The turntable of a record player has a rotary action.

rotate *verb*

rotary bit   *noun*
A rotary bit is part of a **drill**. It is a tool which bores round holes as the drill is turned. It is made up of a hard-ended, steel rod with a deep double, spiral cut down its length. The edge of the spiral is very sharp.
He made a hole in the door with a rotary bit.

rotary engine   *noun*
A rotary engine is a kind of **internal combustion engine**. It has a central part called a rotor, instead of pistons in cylinders. The rotor is made to spin round by the **force** of burning gases. Rotary engines have fewer moving parts than other types of internal combustion engine.
Rotary engines can sometimes be used in cars and motor cycles.

rotary pump   *noun*
A rotary pump is a kind of **pump** which contains **gear wheels**. Liquids are forced between the teeth of the gear wheels and move through the rotary pump as the wheels turn.
Rotary pumps are used to pump thick liquids, such as heavy oil.

rotary vane pump   *noun*
A rotary vane pump is a kind of **pump** which contains vanes like the blades of a fan. The vanes are attached to a shaft. When the shaft turns round, or rotates, the vanes move round and push liquid in front of them.
The shaft of a rotary vane pump can be driven by a petrol, diesel or electric motor.

rotor blades   *plural noun*
Rotor blades are parts of a **helicopter**. They hold the helicopter up in the air and control its take-off and landing. Rotor blades are mounted above the **fuselage** of the helicopter and are driven round by the **engine**. They are sometimes known as a rotary wing.
The rotor blades began to turn, and soon the helicopter took off.

rudder   *noun*
A rudder is a steering device in a **ship** or an **aircraft**. It is a piece of metal which can be turned to the left or right. The ship or aircraft turns in the direction in which the rudder is moved. In a ship, the rudder is under water.
The ship's rudder moved to the right, and the ship steered right.

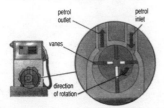

petrol
outlet

petrol
inlet

vanes

direction
of rotation

113

S

safety valve *noun*

A safety valve is a **device** for releasing pressure in a machine. If too much steam is made inside a **boiler**, the safety valve opens to let some of the steam out. Otherwise, the boiler might explode.

A safety valve is designed to work when pressure reaches a certain point.

satellite ► page 115

satellite dish *noun*

A satellite dish is an **aerial**. It collects radio or television signals which have been sent to a **satellite** and are then bounced back to Earth. A satellite dish has to be positioned carefully to point at the satellite.

Signals from a satellite dish flow down wires into a television set.

saw *noun*

A saw is a **device** used for cutting solid materials. It is made up of a blade with triangular teeth cut into one edge, and a handle at one end. Wood saws are much longer than metal saws. They have their teeth bent slightly to left and right, or offset, so they do not stick in the saw cut.

He cut the wood for the fire with a saw.

scale *noun*

A scale is a set of marks which show a measurement. A scale is found on **meters** and some other instruments.

The scale of a barometer is marked in millibars.

scales ► weighing machine

scanner *noun*

A scanner is a machine which looks at, or examines, objects. Part of the scanner moves backwards, forwards and downwards over the object and collects information. This information forms an electronic picture.

A scanner inside a television camera collects information about the scene in front of it.

scan *verb*

scissors *noun*

Scissors are a **device** for cutting. They are a kind of **lever**. They cut by squeezing the material to be cut between two sharp blades.

The hairdresser trimmed her hair with scissors.

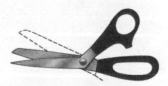

scrambler *noun*

A scrambler is a **device** for keeping messages secret. A scrambler jumbles up **electric signals** so that they can be understood only by someone who has a similar device.

The President used a scrambler to talk by telephone to his generals.

scramble *verb*

screen *noun*

A screen is part of a **television** or a visual display unit. It displays pictures or writing. A screen is made of glass. On the inside, it has a coating of **chemicals** which are sensitive and light up when hit by the beam from an **electron gun**. This forms the image that appears on the screen.

She looked at the screen of her visual display unit to see what she had written.

satellite *noun*

A satellite is an object launched into space
by a **rocket**. Satellites circle, or orbit, the
Earth or another body in space. Earth
satellites are used to observe and forecast
the weather and for **telecommunications**.
*The weather satellite showed that there were
thunderstorms approaching.*

This research satellite studies, or
surveys, the surface of the Earth.
It may look at such features as the
disappearance of the rain forests, or
the wearing away of the coastline of a
particular country.

This type of communications satellite
passes on signals between ground
stations on Earth and spacecraft in
space.

This weather satellite sends
information back to Earth about the
weather. It looks at cloud formations
and helps to forecast severe weather
conditions, such as hurricanes.

115

screw *noun*

A screw is a
fastening device.
It is made of metal.
A screw has a wide
top, called the head,
and a sharp, pointed
end. A spiral groove
called the thread
runs round the body
of the screw. There
is a slot or a cross
on the head, where
the end of a
screwdriver fits to
turn the screw.
*He used a screw to
fix the mirror to the
wall.*
screw *verb*

screw jack *noun*

A screw jack is a lifting device. It is worked
by turning or pulling a handle. The platform
of the jack is placed under the object to be
lifted. When the handle of the jack is moved,
the platform rises on a column which has a
thread or screw running round it.
He used a screw jack to lift the car's wheel.

screwdriver *noun*

A screwdriver is a small tool. It is used to
drive **screws** into wood, metal or other
material. The head has a flat blade or a
cross-shaped blade which matches the slot
or cross cut into the head of the screw.
When the handle of the screwdriver is
turned, the screw is driving in.
*He could not undo the screw because he did
not have a screwdriver small enough.*

seed drill *noun*

A seed drill is a farm machine for planting
seeds. It has a container for the seeds and
lets them out, or releases them, slowly as it
is pulled over a field by a tractor.
*The farmer brought out his seed drill to plant
his barley seeds.*

seismograph *noun*

A seismograph is an instrument for
measuring movements of the Earth's
surface. It is used to record earthquakes.
Pendulum seismographs measure
movements between a pendulum and a
fixed drum and record them on paper.
Electronic seismographs display
movements on a screen.
*The seismograph recorded a small
earthquake.*

semiconductor *noun*

A semiconductor is a kind of material that
conducts **electricity** at a special rate. Most
semiconductors are made from silicon.
Semiconductors are used in many kinds of
electronic equipment.
*A computer is able to work faster with the
help of a semiconductor.*

sensors and detectors ► page 118

sewing machine *noun*

A sewing machine is a machine which
automatically makes stitches in cloth. It is
worked by a handle, a **treadle** or an **electric
motor**. Most sewing machines can make
different kinds of stitch for different
purposes.
*She sat at her sewing machine and carried
on making her new dress.*

shadoof *noun*

A shadoof is a simple machine for raising water. It is a pole with a bucket and a **counterweight**. A shadoof is a kind of **lever**. It is used to water, or irrigate, fields in some hot countries.
The farmer raised water for his crops from the river with a shadoof.

shaft *noun*

1. A shaft is part of a **machine**. It is a rod which turns, or rotates. It is connected to a **wheel** or a **gear**.
Engines, turbines and propellers have shafts.
2. A shaft is a vertical tunnel. Shafts in coal mines carry miners and coal between the coalface and the surface. A **lift** runs up and down inside a mine shaft.
A special lift called a cage carries miners up and down the mine shaft.

shaver *noun*

A shaver is a **device** for removing hair. It has sharp blades which vibrate or rotate behind a grill or metal foil. A shaver is driven by a small **electric motor**.
Her father shaves every morning with an electric shaver.

sheet-feeder *noun*

A sheet-feeder is a **device** which puts one sheet of paper at a time into a **printing machine**. It picks the sheets up and passes them through rollers into the machine.
A printer with a sheet-feeder can be left to work by itself until printing is finished.

ship ► page 120

shock absorber *noun*

A shock absorber is part of a **vehicle**. It has **coil springs** or a **hydraulic system** which take in, or absorb, the shock of bumps and holes in the road surface. Another name for a shock absorber is a damper.
The car's shock absorbers gave them a comfortable ride, even over a bumpy road.

short take-off and landing aircraft
noun

A short take-off and landing aircraft is an **aeroplane** which is designed to use a short runway. It has very large, moveable flaps at the back, and slats on the front of the wings. These allow it to rise or fall steeply and quickly. The abbreviation for short take-off and landing aircraft is STOL.
The short take-off and landing aircraft was able to land safely at a clearing in the jungle.

short-wave radio *noun*

Short-wave radio is a method of **transmitting** and receiving signals by **radio**. A short-wave radio transmitter can send signals all round the world. These signals are bounced back, or reflected, by a part of Earth's atmosphere called the ionosphere.
He listened to a concert broadcast from Australia by short-wave radio.

shutter *noun*

A shutter is a part of a **camera**. It is a set of interlocked metal flaps which open and close. The flaps are fitted between the lens and the film. When the shutter is open, light passes through the **lens** of the camera onto the film. Many cameras have adjustable shutter speeds which can range from one two-thousandth of a second to 30 seconds. Some cameras have electronic shutters that **automatically** adjust speeds.
The shutter can be set to open for different lengths of time for different amounts of light.

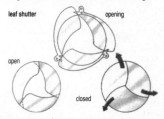

leaf shutter — opening — open — closed

sensors and detectors   *nouns*

Sensors and detectors are **devices** which react to certain events which are called stimuli. Sensors in a **robot** allow it to find the correct position for it to do work. A **smoke detector** gives a warning if fire breaks out. *Burglar alarm systems contain sensors and detectors.*

One type of burglar alarm gives out, or emits, rays called microwaves. The microwaves detect movement anywhere in the room and trigger an alarm bell.

Another type of burglar alarm emits ultrasonic rays. They detect the slightest sound made by a person entering the room.

A third type of burglar alarm emits infra-red rays. These detect the body heat given off by someone entering the room.

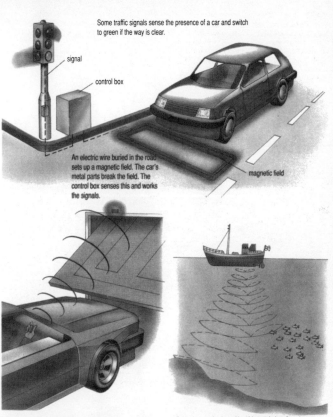

Some traffic signals sense the presence of a car and switch to green if the way is clear.

signal

control box

An electric wire buried in the road sets up a magnetic field. The car's metal parts break the field. The control box senses this and works the signals.

magnetic field

Some garage doors can be opened and closed automatically. The driver points a remote control unit at the door and presses a button.

Sonar is a method used by ships and aircraft to detect objects underwater. Some fishing boats use sonar to find schools of fish.

119

ship *noun*

A ship is a large **boat** which goes to sea.
There are many different kinds of ship. For
hundreds of years, all ships had sails and
were powered by the wind. Today they
usually have **steam turbines** or **diesel
engines**. Some ships are **nuclear**-powered.
*A cargo ship carries raw materials and
goods from one port to another.*

This Spanish galleon was used in the early 1600s
as a trading and fighting ship.

The ss Great Britain was the first propeller-driven
ship to cross the Atlantic in 1845.

This picture of the Queen Elizabeth II passenger liner has been cut away to show the main areas.

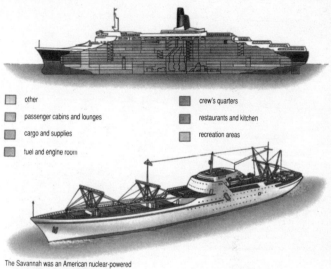

	other		crew's quarters
	passenger cabins and lounges		restaurants and kitchen
	cargo and supplies		recreation areas
	fuel and engine room		

The Savannah was an American nuclear-powered merchant ship launched in 1959.

This oil tanker was built to carry petroleum from oil terminals.

shuttle *noun*

A shuttle is a part of a **loom**. It carries one of the threads which are being woven and passes it over and under the other, vertical thread.
Several different shuttles are used in a loom which is weaving cloth with a coloured pattern.

signal *noun*

1. A signal is a message. **Electric signals** can be sent along wires or through the air using **radio**. Telephone calls and radio and television programmes are made up of signals.
We could not get a clear picture on the television because lightning disturbed the signal.

2. A signal is a **device** used to show whether a road or railway is safe to be used. Most signals use lights coloured red for danger, green for safe and amber or yellow for caution.
The train driver stopped because the signal showed red.

silencer *noun*

A silencer is a device which makes **engines** run quietly. It passes **exhaust gases** through a series of pipes lined with a special material. The material takes in, or absorbs, sound. All vehicles, such as motorcars and motor cycles, are fitted with a silencer.
The car made a loud noise because it had a hole in its silencer.

silicon chip *noun*

A silicon chip is a kind of crystal. It is made from a tiny piece of a material called silicon. A silicon chip has **electric circuits** cut, or etched, on it. A silicon chip is surrounded by a plastic case to protect it from damage. There are many silicon chips contained in a **computer**.
Some silicon chips are only two millimetres square.

simulator ► **flight simulator**

simple machines ► page 124

single lens reflex camera *noun*

A single lens reflex, or SLR, camera is a **camera** which has a special viewfinder. When you look through the viewfinder, you see exactly what will be in the photograph you are going to take. Prisms and a mirror bend, or reflect, the light waves onto the viewfinder lens.
You cannot see through the viewfinder of a single lens reflex camera while the picture is being taken.

siphon *noun*

A siphon is a **device** for moving liquids from one container to another. It is a curved tube or pipe. One end of the siphon must be placed in the liquid to be moved and the other end in a container at a lower level than the liquid. If the siphon is full of liquid to start with, it will allow the higher container to empty into the lower.
He used a siphon to empty the petrol out of the car's petrol tank.

skate *noun*

A skate is a frame with a blade or wheels fixed to a shoe. Ice skates have blades that allow a person to glide over ice. Ice skating is an Olympic sport. Roller skates have small wheels and can be used on any smooth, hard surface. People wearing skates can travel very fast.
She put on her ice skates and glided over the frozen lake.

skate *verb*

skip lorry *noun*

A skip lorry is a **vehicle** designed to carry containers, called skips, full of rubbish. It has a crane which lifts the skip onto a platform behind the driver's cab. The skip lorry then takes the full skip to a refuse site where its contents are dumped.
The builders put the broken bricks into a skip which was collected by the skip lorry to be taken to the refuse tip.

sled *noun*
A sled is a wooden frame which is designed to move downhill across snow or ice. Boards are mounted on runners which slide smoothly over the surface causing little **friction**. The passenger rides on the boards.
She guided the sled down the slope using her body weight and her arms to steer it.

slide projector *noun*
A slide projector is an **appliance** which shows still pictures on a **screen**. The pictures are projected from special photographs called transparencies. These allow a bright light to shine through to a **lens** which throws the picture onto the screen.
They showed us some photographs of their holiday on their slide projector.

SLR camera ► single lens reflex camera

smelting *noun*
Smelting describes how metals are obtained from metal ores. The ore is heated in a **furnace** and the metal is separated from the waste, or **slag**.
Smelting is done in a foundry.

smoke detector ► sensors and detectors

snow blower *noun*
A snow blower is a **vehicle** which clears snow. It has a fan which sends out a stream of air. This blows the snow to each side.
The airport was closed until a snow blower had cleared the runways.

socket *noun*
1. A socket is a **device** with holes in it. The holes fit the terminals on an electric plug.
An appliance is connected to the electricity supply by pushing a plug into a socket.
2. A socket is a part of some machines. It is a hollow into which another part fits and is held in place, but is free to move.
The gear lever fitted into the gearbox socket.

software *noun*
Software is the **data** and **programs** that a **computer** uses. Software is loaded into the computer's **hardware**. It may be on **floppy disks** or **magnetic tape**.
Software gives a computer instructions on what work to do and the information with which to work.

solar heater *noun*
A solar heater is a **device** which heats water by using **energy** from the Sun. The energy is collected by **solar panels** mounted on the roof of a building. The solar panels contain water. A **pump** sends the heated water to a boiler and radiators.
The solar heater kept the house warm in winter.

solar panel *noun*
A solar panel is a device for collecting energy from the Sun for use in a **solar heater**. It contains metal pipes under a glass or plastic screen.
Solar panels are mounted on the roofs of buildings facing the Sun.

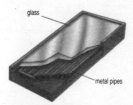
glass

metal pipes

solenoid *noun*
A solenoid is a part of an **electromagnet**. It is a coil of wire wound round an iron bar. When **electric current** flows through a solenoid, it creates a magnetic force. This force can operate other devices. Solenoids are found in **relays** and electric doors.
A solenoid was used to operate the level crossing gates.

simple machines *noun*

A simple machine is a **device** that does work. It lessens the amount of **effort** needed for work to be done. As with all machines, a simple machine needs a source of **energy** for it to work.

The six simple machines are a screw, a wedge, an inclined plane, a pulley, a lever and a wheel and axle.

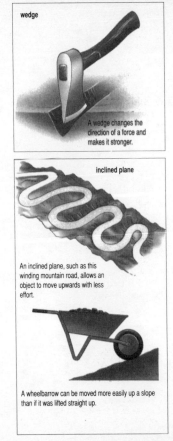

wedge

A wedge changes the direction of a force and makes it stronger.

inclined plane

An inclined plane, such as this winding mountain road, allows an object to move upwards with less effort.

A wheelbarrow can be moved more easily up a slope than if it was lifted straight up.

screw

A screw is a simple machine that has a ridge, called a thread, cut around it. The effort needed to turn a screw is much less than the force with which it moves forward.

pulley

A pulley is a simple machine made up of wheels and ropes. It changes the direction of the pull, or lifting force. It is easier to pull down on something than to lift it up.

lever

A lever is a bar or rod that moves round a fulcrum. The effort of pressing down on one end lifts a load.

wheel and axle

A wheel and axle is a part of many machines. It can pass, or transmit, a turning motion from one part of a machine to another.

solid fuel rocket   *noun*

A solid fuel rocket is a rocket engine which burns fuel that is solid. A firework rocket is a solid fuel rocket. Its fuel is a kind of gunpowder.
The sailors sent up an alarm signal by using a solid fuel rocket.

sonar   *noun*

Sonar is a device which is fitted to some **ships**. It works in a similar way to **radar**. Sonar is used to find objects under water. It gives out very high-pitched sound waves which are bounced back, or reflected, by the objects.
The fishermen used sonar to find shoals of fish.

sound recorder   *noun*

A sound recorder is an **appliance** which records sound reaching it through a **microphone**. Most sound recorders use **magnetic tape**, but some record on **discs**.
He read his story into a sound recorder and then listened to his own voice.

space probe   *noun*

A space probe is a **spacecraft** which does not carry a crew. It is used to explore space. Space probes carry cameras and many different kinds of instrument to study the planets they visit. A space probe sends information back to Earth by **radio waves**.
The space probe was sent into orbit round the planet Venus.

space shuttle   *noun*

A space shuttle is a kind of **spacecraft**. It travels to and fro between the Earth and space. A space shuttle can carry astronauts and equipment to a space station in orbit. When a space shuttle returns to Earth, it lands on a runway at a speed of approximately 320 kilometres per hour.
The space shuttle carried a new crew out to the space station.

space station   *noun*

A space station is a spacecraft which stays in space for a long time. It is a **satellite**. Space stations are used to carry out research. Their crews can be exchanged by using a **space shuttle**.
Scientists hope to build a space station which can hold up to 30 people.

spacecraft   *noun*

A spacecraft is a **vehicle** which is sent into space. It may have a crew or it may be unmanned. Some spacecraft are sent into orbit round the Earth or another of the planets. Others make short journeys and return to Earth.
There was a roar from the rocket engine and the spacecraft lifted off.

spanner   *noun*

A spanner is a tool which is used to turn a **nut** or **bolt**. It has a notch cut in the end which is the same size as the nut or the head of the bolt. Spanners are made of **steel**.
He used a spanner to tighten the saddle nut on his bicycle.

spark plug   *noun*

A spark plug is a part of some **internal combustion engines**. It fits into each of the **cylinders**. When it receives an electric current, it makes a spark which sets alight, or ignites, the mixture of fuel and air in the cylinder.
The car engine was not firing properly because its spark plugs were dirty.

spectacles *plural noun*
Spectacles are devices which help people with poor sight to see more clearly. They are two **lenses** held in place in a frame. They re-focus the image on the lens of the eye.
He could not read the paper because he had forgotten his spectacles.

speed trap ► radar speed trap

speedometer *noun*
A speedometer is part of a **vehicle**. It shows how fast the vehicle is travelling. A land vehicle speedometer is connected by a cable and gears to the **transmission**. It shows measurements on a **dial**.
The speedometer showed that the car was travelling far too fast.

spin drier *noun*
A spin drier is an **appliance** used in the home. It dries wet washing by spinning it fast inside a drum. The water is thrown out of the drum by **centrifugal force**. A heater finishes the drying process.
When she had washed the clothes, she put them in the spin drier.

spindle *noun*
1. A spindle is a metal rod on which part of a machine turns round, or rotates.
An axle is a kind of spindle.
2. A spindle is part of a **spinning machine**. It is a metal pin used for twisting and winding the thread.
The spindles on the spinning machine were full of thread ready for weaving.

spinning machine *noun*
A spinning machine is a machine for making yarn or thread out of **raw material**. It straightens out the fibres of the raw material and then twists them together evenly, forming a long string or yarn.
At the factory there was a spinning machine making woollen yarn from sheep's wool.

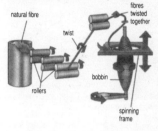

natural fibre

twist

rollers

bobbin

fibres twisted together

spinning frame

spirit level *noun*
A spirit level is a **tool**. It is used to make sure that a surface is level. A spirit level contains a glass or plastic tube. Inside the tube is a liquid with a bubble of air in it. The spirit level is placed on the surface to be checked. If the bubble is exactly in the centre of the tube, the surface is level.
The builder used a spirit level to check that the floor did not slope.

spring *noun*
A spring is a part of many machines. It may be a coil or a bar made of special spring steel. Springs return to their original form if they are pushed out of shape. The **axles** of vehicles have springs fitted to them to make them travel more smoothly. If the **wheel** of a car goes over a bump, the springs that are positioned between the body of the car and the wheels absorb the shock. This stops the passengers from feeling a sharp bump.
His bicycle saddle was uncomfortable because one of the springs had broken.
spring *verb*

127

spring balance   *noun*
A spring balance is a kind of **weighing machine**. It contains a **coil spring** which is fixed at the top. The object to be weighed is hung on a hook at the lower end of the spring. A needle is pulled down along a **scale** and shows the weight of the object.
He used a spring balance to find the weight of the fruit.

sprinkler ▶ lawn sprinkler

sprinkler system   *noun*
A sprinkler system is a method of putting out a fire. It is found in many buildings, such as large stores. The system contains **fire detectors**. If any of these detect a fire, the sprinklers are turned on **automatically**. They spread a fine spray of water over the danger area and put out the fire.
The fire in the factory did little damage because the sprinkler system put it out.

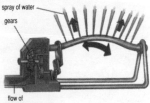

spray of water

gears

flow of
water

sprocket   *noun*
A sprocket is part of a machine. Sprockets are pointed teeth on the outside edge of a **wheel**. They join, or mesh, with the links of a chain. When one wheel turns, its sprockets move the chain and the chain moves another wheel with sprockets. The distance between the sprocket's teeth must be the same as the distance between the chain links. The distance is called the pitch of the sprocket.
Sprockets on the pedal wheel of a bicycle grip the chain and make the rear wheel turn.

spur gears   *plural noun*
Spur gears are parts of some machines. They are used when a **drive shaft** makes another shaft turn at the same angle.
The teeth of spur gears are cut so that they are parallel with the shaft.

spy satellite   *noun*
A spy satellite is a **satellite** in orbit round the Earth. It is used by one country to find out what is happening in another. Television cameras on the spy satellite take pictures which are sent back to Earth.
The spy satellite showed that there was a large army in the desert.

stabilizer   *noun*
A stabilizer is a device fitted to many **ships**. It helps to stop a ship rolling in heavy seas. Stabilizers are shaped like fins and are fitted in pairs, one on each side of the ship, below the water line. Each fin can be tilted **automatically** so that the ship is not affected by the action of the waves.
They had a pleasant voyage because the ship was fitted with stabilizers.

stapler   *noun*
A stapler is a device for fastening things together. A staple is a short length of wire. It is used with a staple gun. The gun pushes the staple in hard. A stapler used for paper bends the ends of the staple over, once it is in place.
She bound the separate pages of her book together with a staple.

starter motor   *noun*
A starter motor is a part of a **vehicle**. It provides a surge of power through a **gear wheel** to turn the **crankshaft** and start the engine. A starter motor is driven by electricity from the vehicle's battery.
My car would not start because there was not enough energy in the battery to turn the starter motor.

static electricity   *noun*
Static electricity is a kind of natural **energy**. It builds up when **electrons** move from one object to another object. It does not flow steadily like an **electric current**. Static electricity stays still or leaps between objects.
Lightning is caused by static electricity leaping between clouds or between a cloud and the ground.

stator   *noun*
A stator is a part of a machine. It is an **electromagnet** inside an **electric motor** or a **generator**. A stator stays still while coils of wire spin round it.
The movement of the coils round the stator generates electricity.

steam engine   *noun*
A steam engine is a kind of **engine** which produces **energy** from boiling water. The pressure of steam from the boiling water is used to drive a **piston**, which in turn can drive wheels or operate machinery.
We had a ride on a railway train pulled by a steam engine.

steam locomotive ► **steam engine**

steam roller   *noun*
A steam roller is a machine which is used to make or mend roads. It is driven by a **steam engine**. At the front, in place of wheels, it has a heavy roller which presses on the road surface and makes it hard. The rear wheels are also heavy rollers.
The road gang used a steam roller to give the road a new top surface.

steam turbine   *noun*
A steam turbine is a kind of **steam engine**. Steam is made by boiling water and forcing it at high pressure through a set of **turbine wheels**. These have slits between them. The force of the steam makes the turbine wheels turn and drive a **shaft**.
Some ships are powered by steam turbines.

steel   *noun*
Steel is a metal which is made by mixing **iron** with other substances. It is made in a **furnace**. Many different kinds of steel are used in machines.
Stainless steel is a kind of steel which does not become rusty.

steel convertor   *noun*
A steel convertor is a piece of equipment for making **steel**. It melts **iron** in a vessel and pumps air through the molten metal. This makes impure substances float to the surface. When the steel is pure enough, the vessel is tipped and the steel is poured into moulds.
Many different kinds of steel can be made in a steel convertor.

steering   *noun*
Steering describes the way that a **vehicle**, **ship** or **aircraft** is made to change direction. A road vehicle is steered by turning a steering wheel connected by **gears** to the front wheels. Ships and aircraft are steered by using a **rudder**. Bicycles and motorcycles are steered by turning the handlebars.
The racing car had excellent steering .
steer   *verb*

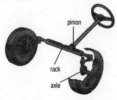

pinion

rack

axle

submarine *noun*

A submarine is a kind of **boat**. It can travel on or under the surface of the water. A submarine contains tanks which are filled with water to make it sink. Most submarines are **warships** and fire **torpedoes** or **nuclear weapons**. Some submarines can travel underwater for many months.

They watched as the submarine filled its tanks with water and dived.

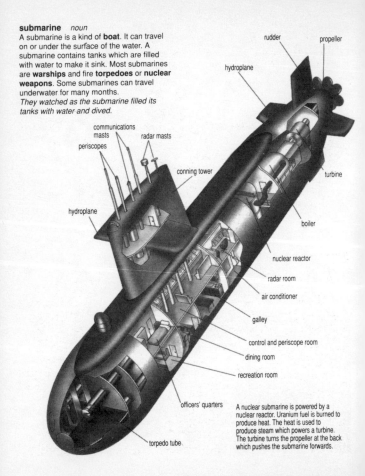

rudder

propeller

hydroplane

communications masts

radar masts

periscopes

conning tower

turbine

hydroplane

boiler

nuclear reactor

radar room

air conditioner

galley

control and periscope room

dining room

recreation room

officers' quarters

torpedo tube

A nuclear submarine is powered by a nuclear reactor. Uranium fuel is burned to produce heat. The heat is used to produce steam which powers a turbine. The turbine turns the propeller at the back which pushes the submarine forwards.

A submersible is a small submarine. It is used by scientists to explore the deep parts of the ocean. It can also be used to take divers down to the sea-bed to repair underwater pipelines.

How a submarine dives and surfaces

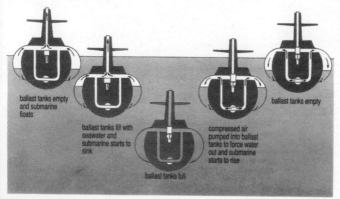

ballast tanks empty and submarine floats

ballast tanks fill with seawater and submarine starts to sink

ballast tanks full

compressed air pumped into ballast tanks to force water out and submarine starts to rise

ballast tanks empty

steering damper   *noun*
A steering damper is a kind of **shock
absorber** fitted to a road **vehicle**. It stops
the steering wheel jerking if the vehicle is
travelling over a rough surface. A steering
damper may be **hydraulic** or a spring.
*The steering dampers made the car easy to
drive.*

stereo-   *prefix*
Stereo- describes things that are made to
seem real or solid. Sounds from a
stereophonic record, tape or radio broadcast
come from different loudspeakers. A
stereoscope allows us to view a picture
which has depth as well as height and width.
*Human beings have two eyes which give
them stereoscopic vision.*

stethoscope   *noun*
A stethoscope is an instrument used by
doctors. It allows them to hear the beating of
the heart and the sound of air in the lungs.
A stethoscope is a tube with an earpiece at
one end. At the other end, a device with a
sensor is placed against the body.
*The doctor listened to her lungs with a
stethoscope.*

stopwatch   *noun*
A stopwatch is a special kind of watch which
can be started or stopped at any time. It is
used to time races and other sports events.
Some stopwatches have a **clockwork
motor**. Others have **electronic** parts.
*Some stopwatches are so accurate that they
can measure hundredths of a second.*

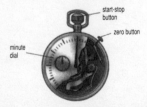

start-stop
button

zero button

minute
dial

streamlined   *adjective*
Streamlined describes the shape of some
objects. Streamlined surfaces are curved, so
that air or water can flow over them easily.
*Submarines, aeroplanes and most motor
cars have streamlined shapes.*

structure   *noun*
A structure is an object which has been built.
Bridges, buildings, tunnels, towers and oil
rigs are some kinds of structure. Some
structures, like houses, enclose people.
Other structures support things. For
example, pillars support a statue. Structures
can also span things, like a bridge that
spans from one side of a river to the other.
*The structure being built in the city centre is
a new office block.*

submarine   ► page 130

submersible   *noun*
A submersible is a very small kind of
submarine. It is used to carry out
underwater repairs to **oil rigs** and other
structures. Submersibles are often fitted with
robots and other tools which can be
operated from inside.
*Two men in a submersible went down to
examine the damage to the oil rig.*

sump   *noun*
A sump is part of a machine. It is a store of a
liquid called **lubricant**. The lubricant is
pumped from the sump to the other parts of
the machine where it is needed.
*When he put oil in his car, the oil ran down
the filler pipe into the sump.*

sun gear   ► planetary gears

superheated   *adjective*
Superheated describes a liquid or gas which
is heated to a very high pressure. The liquid
or gas can then be used to drive an **engine**
or a **turbine**.
*Steam locomotives are powered by
superheated steam.*

supermarket checkout *noun*

A supermarket checkout is the place in a supermarket where you pay for what you have bought. It has an electronic **till** which adds up the amount you have to pay. The checkout may also have **EPOS** equipment. This keeps a check on goods in stock in the supermarket.

The till at the supermarket checkout produced a list of what she had bought.

supersonic *adjective*

Supersonic describes speed. A supersonic speed is faster than the speed of sound. This is about 1,080 kilometres per hour, depending on how dense and humid the air is.

Concorde is a supersonic airliner.

swing-wing aircraft *noun*

Swing-wing aircraft are **aeroplanes**. Their wings can swing backwards or forwards during flight. The wings swing forwards for take-off or landing. In level flight, they swing backwards so they become **streamlined** and air flows more easily over them.

Many fighters are swing-wing aircraft.

wings in forward position

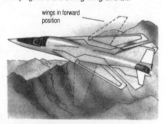

synthesizer *noun*

A synthesizer is a musical instrument. It uses **electronics** and **computers** to produce many different kinds of sound. A synthesizer is played by using a **keyboard**.

The pop group included two electric guitars and a synthesizer.

synthetic *adjective*

Synthetic describes things which are made by people and are not natural. Cotton is a natural fibre, but nylon is a synthetic one. **Plastics** are synthetic materials.

Her new dress was made from a mixture of natural and synthetic fibres.

syringe *noun*

A syringe is a kind of **pump**. It is a **cylinder** containing a **piston**. There is a nozzle at one end and a small handle at the other. Liquid is drawn into the cylinder through the nozzle and then pushed out again. Doctors often use syringes to give people medicines.

The doctor used a syringe to give me an injection to prevent hay fever.

tanker *noun*

1. A tanker is a kind of **ship**. It carries large amounts of a liquid cargo. Some tankers carry **petroleum** or petroleum products.
They went to watch the oil tanker docking at the oil terminal.

2. A tanker is a road vehicle which carries a load such as oil, flour or sugar. The load is carried in a large tank behind the driver's cab.
The tanker delivered a fresh supply of petrol to the filling station.

tap *noun*

A tap is a **device** for controlling the flow of liquids. It is a kind of **valve**. When a tap is turned on, it allows the liquid to flow out. The flow is stopped when the tap is turned off.
She turned on the hot and cold water taps to fill the bath.

tap *verb*

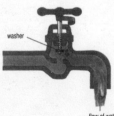

washer

flow of water

tape ► magnetic tape

tape head *noun*

A tape head is a part of a **tape recorder**. When the tape recorder is recording or playing, **magnetic tape** is pressed against the tape head. **Electric signals** pass from the tape through the head to the amplifier.
You can buy a special tape which cleans the tape heads of a tape recorder.

tape recorder ► page 135

telecommunications *plural noun*

Telecommunications is the way people communicate with each other using **electric signals**. It began with the invention of the **telegraph**. The telegraph marked the beginning of the telecommunications age that is known today. Telecommunications can travel by **radio waves**, along wires or along optical **fibre optic** cables.
Radio, television, the telephone and fax machines are different kinds of telecommunications.

telegraph *noun*

A telegraph is a **device** for sending messages over long distances. The messages are sent along a wire in a **code**, which is made up of long and short bursts of electricity. The operator taps out these bursts with a key or finger pad. Telegraph messages are received by a **loudspeaker** or on a paper tape as a series of short and long signals.
The soldiers sent back a report from the battlefield by telegraph.

telephone *noun*

A telephone is an instrument for communicating over a distance. When someone speaks into the mouthpiece of a telephone, the sounds are changed into **electric signals**. These travel along a wire or **fibre optic** cable to the person at the other end. Then the signals are changed back into sound.
She had some important news to tell her friend, so she used the telephone.

tape recorder *noun*

A tape recorder is a machine. It records
electric signals on **magnetic tape**. The
signals can make up sounds, pictures or
computer programs. A tape recorder can
also play back the signals to a loudspeaker,
television set or computer.
*He listened to the sound of his own voice on
his tape recorder.*

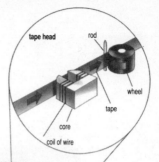

cassette tape recorder

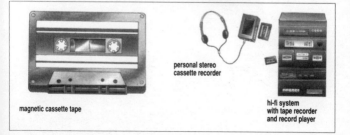

magnetic cassette tape

personal stereo
cassette recorder

hi-fi system
with tape recorder
and record player

telephoto lens *noun*

A telephoto lens is a **device** which can be fitted to a **camera**. It is made up of a number of **lenses**. A telephoto lens is used to take a close-up photograph of a distant object. It works like a telescope and makes objects seem larger and nearer.

He used a telephoto lens to take a photograph of the distant shore.

teleprinter *noun*

A teleprinter is a machine for sending and receiving printed messages. A message is put into a teleprinter using a **keyboard**. The teleprinter changes the message into **electric signals** and sends them along wires or by radio. Another teleprinter changes the signals back into letters and numbers and prints them on paper.

Newspaper reporters often use teleprinters to send reports back to their newspaper offices.

telescope ▶ page 138

teletext *noun*

Teletext is printed information which appears on a television screen. It is sent from the **transmitter**, together with ordinary television pictures, but it is hidden from view above and below the screen. A device called a decoder is needed to bring teletext information into view on the screen.

Teletext showed us a list of what was on at all the cinemas and theatres in the city.

television ▶ page 140

television camera *noun*

A television camera is a special **camera** which is used to take television pictures. It contains **electron guns**. These scan the scene in front of the camera and turn light and colours into **electric signals**. These signals are sent down a wire to a **transmitter**.

In a television play, several television cameras are used to show the action.

television receiver *noun*

A television receiver is an **appliance** which receives and shows **television** programmes. It collects **electric signals** from an **aerial** and changes them into pictures and sound. The electric signals make an **electron gun** fire **electrons** at the television screen as the electrons hit. Pictures are shown on a screen and the sounds are heard on a loudspeaker.

Most families own one television receiver.

television satellite *noun*

A television satellite is a **satellite** which stays over the same part of the Earth's surface. It receives television signals from a **transmitter** and sends them back to Earth.

Television satellites are used to show events which are happening on the other side of the world.

telex *noun*

Telex is a form of **telecommunications**. It is a way of sending messages using teleprinters. These are linked together by telephone lines.

He sent a telex message to say when he would be arriving in New York.

temperature gauge *noun*

A temperature gauge is a **device** which shows the temperature of a liquid, solid or gas. It shows the temperature on a **dial**. Many machines are fitted with temperature gauges to make sure that they do not overheat or become too cold.

The temperature gauge showed that the water in the car engine was nearly boiling.

tension *noun*

Tension is a kind of **force** that tries to stretch an object. There is tension in a string that is being pulled down by a weight. The opposite of tension is compression.

Tension in the spokes keeps the round shape of a bicycle wheel.

terminal *noun*

1. A terminal is a special dock where **petroleum** or petroleum products are unloaded and stored.

The oil tanker docked at the terminal and unloaded its cargo.

2. A terminal is part of an **electric circuit**. It connects a device to the electricity supply. A battery has a negative and a positive terminal. Bulb holders and most switches have two terminals.

He screwed the electric wires into the terminals.

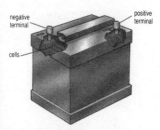

negative terminal
positive terminal
cells

thermometer *noun*

A thermometer is an instrument which measures temperature. Most thermometers have a liquid inside a thin, glass tube. When the liquid is warmed, it expands and rises up the tube. The temperature shows on a **scale**.

The doctor slipped a thermometer under her tongue and took her temperature.

thermonuclear weapon ► **nuclear weapon**

thermostat *noun*

A thermostat is a **device** which controls a **boiler** or a **heater**. It can be set to switch the boiler or heater off when a certain temperature is reached. Then it switches it on again when the temperature falls. A thermostat contains a thin strip of metal. When the strip heats up, it bends and works a switch.

If the temperature falls, a thermostat automatically switches on the heater.

throttle *noun*

A throttle is a part of an **engine**. It is a **valve** which controls the amount of fuel and air flowing into the engine. Opening the throttle makes the engine give out more power.

He put his foot down on the throttle to make the car go faster.

thruster ► **after-burner**

ticket machine *noun*

A ticket machine is a machine which **automatically** issues tickets when money is placed in it. Ticket machines are found at some railway stations and car parks.

He bought a ticket for the journey from a ticket machine.

tidal power *noun*

Tidal power is **energy** produced by the rise and fall of the sea's tides. The flow of water can be used to drive a **turbine** and make **electricity**.

There is a tidal power station at Rance, in France.

telescope *noun*

A telescope is an **optical instrument**. It is used to study the night sky. It contains **lenses** and **mirrors** which make distant objects look closer.

You can see the 'mountains of the Moon' clearly if you look at the Moon through a telescope.

This portable telescope has a 50-millimetre lens and magnifies objects 150 times.

This 400-centimetre telescope is one of the most advanced radio telescopes in the world. It is at Mount Palomar Observatory, in the United States of America.

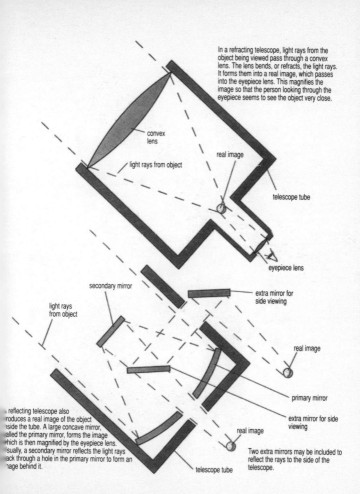

In a refracting telescope, light rays from the object being viewed pass through a convex lens. The lens bends, or refracts, the light rays. It forms them into a real image, which passes into the eyepiece lens. This magnifies the image so that the person looking through the eyepiece seems to see the object very close.

convex lens

light rays from object

real image

telescope tube

eyepiece lens

secondary mirror

extra mirror for side viewing

light rays from object

real image

primary mirror

extra mirror for side viewing

real image

A reflecting telescope also produces a real image of the object inside the tube. A large concave mirror, called the primary mirror, forms the image which is then magnified by the eyepiece lens. Usually, a secondary mirror reflects the light rays back through a hole in the primary mirror to form an image behind it.

Two extra mirrors may be included to reflect the rays to the side of the telescope.

telescope tube

139

television *noun*

Television is a method of sending and receiving sounds and pictures over a distance. It uses **radio waves** to carry **electric signals**.

Television is the main source of entertainment for most people.

Electronic circuits change electric signals into sound, which comes out through a loudspeaker.

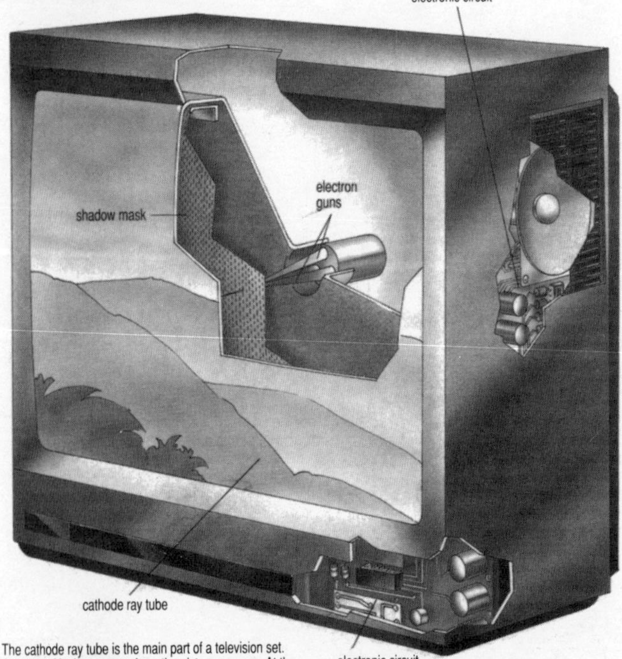

electronic circuit

shadow mask

electron guns

cathode ray tube

electronic circuit

The cathode ray tube is the main part of a television set. At one end is the screen where the picture appears. At the other end, electron guns shoot electrons at the screen to make the picture.

There is a metal shadow mask behind the television screen, with rows of holes punched in it. The screen is coated with tiny dots of phosphor, arranged in groups of three. The dots glow green, blue and red when electrons are fired at them. Three electron guns fire electrons through the holes in the shadow mask, so that each gun lights up the right colour.

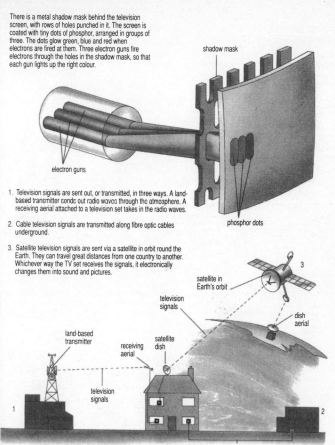

electron guns

shadow mask

phosphor dots

1. Television signals are sent out, or transmitted, in three ways. A land-based transmitter sends out radio waves through the atmosphere. A receiving aerial attached to a television set takes in the radio waves.

2. Cable television signals are transmitted along fibre optic cables underground.

3. Satellite television signals are sent via a satellite in orbit round the Earth. They can travel great distances from one country to another. Whichever way the TV set receives the signals, it electronically changes them into sound and pictures.

satellite in Earth's orbit

television signals

dish aerial

land-based transmitter

receiving aerial

satellite dish

television signals

fibre optic cable carrying TV signals

1

2

till *noun*

A till is a machine which is found in shops. Some tills work out how much a customer has to pay and how much change is to be given. Tills provide printed receipts from a roll of paper. Another name for a till is a cash register.

The shop assistant put the money in the till and gave me the change and a receipt.

tin *noun*

Tin is a **chemical** element. It is a soft, silvery metal which has a low melting point. Tin is used to make solder to join metal parts together. It is also used to coat **steel** which is to be made into cans for food.

Tinplate is steel which has been given a coating of tin.

titanium *noun*

Titanium is a **chemical** element. It is a very hard metal that stands up to high temperatures. It is added to **steel** to make parts of an **aircraft** which become very hot. Titanium does not rust or corrode easily.

Many of the jet engine's parts were made of titanium steel.

toaster *noun*

A toaster is an **appliance** for toasting bread. It contains wires which are heated by an **electric current**. The bread is placed close to the wires. When the toast is ready, a spring makes it pop up and switches off the current.

He made them each a slice of toast in the toaster.

toboggan *noun*

A toboggan is a long, narrow **sled** usually made from wood or a hard **plastic**. It is used to travel downhill on a snow-covered slope. The base of the toboggan is flat and smooth and the front curves upwards. Unlike a sled, it has no runners. This helps reduce **friction** as the toboggan slides forwards.

Toboggan races form part of the Winter Olympic Games.

tool *noun*

A tool is a device for carrying out a particular task. **Hammers**, **planes**, **spanners** and **screwdrivers** are tools. Tools powered by motors are called power tools. **Electric drills** and **circular saws** are power tools.

The mechanic kept all his tools in a tool chest so that he could carry them about.

torpedo *noun*

A torpedo is a weapon fired at sea by a **warship**. It has its own **motor**. A torpedo is fired underwater towards the hull of an enemy ship. When it reaches its target, a warhead in the nose of the torpedo explodes.

Many enemy ships were sunk by torpedoes fired by submarines.

torque *noun*

Torque is a word which describes the **force** an engine uses to turn a shaft. A large torque is needed to start an engine moving. Once it is moving, less torque is needed to keep it going. A vehicle uses torque from its engine to turn the wheels.

The heavy lorry needed a large torque to start pulling away from the roadside.

tower crane *noun*

A tower crane is a kind of **crane** used on building sites. It is a tall, metal tower with a crossbar, or jib, at the top. The crane driver can swing the jib in any direction. Cables hang from one end of the jib and there is a **counterweight** at the other end.

The tower crane lifted slabs of concrete and put them in place.

track *noun*

1. A track is a collection of rails and **points** on a railway line.

The railway train came quickly down the track.

2. A track is a place where events such as car and motor cycle races are held.

The racing car skidded and came off the track.

142

traction engine   *noun*

A traction engine is a road vehicle which is driven by a **steam engine**. It can be used in two ways. Traction engines may be used to pull wagons, **ploughs** or other machines along roads or over fields. They can also operate machines if the drive of the traction engine is connected by an endless belt to the machine.

Traction engines are often shown at rallies.

tractor ▶ page 144

traffic lights   *plural noun*

Traffic lights are **signals**. They tell road users when it is safe to move on. They show a red light for danger, green for safety and an amber light which means caution. Traffic lights are usually found on busy roads in towns and cities.

The traffic lights were red, so the bus stopped.

train   *noun*

A train is a vehicle which runs along a **track**. It is usually made up of several coaches or wagons. Trains are pulled or pushed by locomotives powered by **steam engines**, **diesel engines** or **electric motors**. They are often used for carrying passengers and moving heavy cargo, or freight. Trains may also be used beneath the streets in underground railways or subways.

We went to the railway station to catch the early train.

transceiver   *noun*

A transceiver is a **device** with an **aerial**, which can both **transmit** and receive messages by **radio**. It is small enough to fit into a pocket. Police and other emergency services often use transceivers to relay and receive important messages. *At the scene of the accident, the policeman took his transceiver out of his pocket and spoke to headquarters.*

transducer   *noun*

A transducer is a **device** which changes **energy** from one form to another. A microphone is a transducer because it changes sound energy into electrical energy. Phototransistors, light bulbs, loudspeakers and solenoids are some other kinds of transducer.

All forms of telecommunications rely on transducers to make them work.

transformer   *noun*

A transformer is a **device** which makes an **electric current** stronger or weaker. It is made of two separate coils of wire which are wound onto an iron core.

The transformer decreased the current from the power station from 15,000 volts to 240 volts.

transistor   *noun*

A transistor is an **electronic** device. It is made from a material called silicon. Transistors have three wires attached to them. They can change the strength or direction of **electric signals**.

Radios, television sets and record-players all contain transisiors.

tractor   *noun*

A tractor is a **vehicle** which is used mainly
on farms. It can do many different jobs.
Tractors can pull **wagons** and farm machines
such as **ploughs**. With **power take-off** they
can also provide energy for other machines.
*The farmer connected his tractor to a plough
and set off to plough his land.*

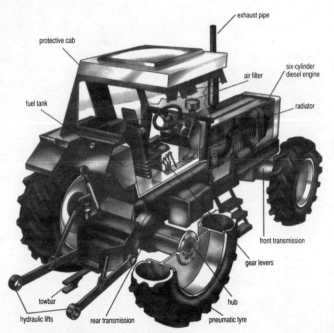

exhaust pipe

protective cab

air filter

six-cylinder
diesel engine

fuel tank

radiator

front transmission

gear levers

towbar

hub

hydraulic lifts

rear transmission

pneumatic tyre

A tractor has large rear wheels to keep it steady on rough ground.
Its tyres have deep treads to grip well in muddy fields.

144

transmission *noun*

A transmission is part of a **vehicle** driven by an **engine**. It is made up of **gears**. The transmission sends, or **transmits**, energy from the engine's drive **shaft** to the road wheels.

The car's transmission was faulty and it broke down.

transmit *verb*

Transmit means to carry or send something from one place to another. In a car, **energy** is transmitted from the engine to the driving wheels. A **radio transmitter** transmits **electric signals** to **radio receivers**.

A telephone transmits and receives voice messages.

transmitter *noun*

A transmitter is a device which sends out **electric signals** by means of **radio waves**. Radio and television signals come from transmitters. A television **antenna** receives radio waves from a transmitter. These waves are turned into electric signals. A tuner picks a signal which is then amplified and split into picture and sound signals.

The radio signals that we picked up were very faint because we were a long way from the transmitter.

treadle *noun*

A treadle is a part of a machine which uses human muscle power. A person places their foot on the treadle and presses it up and down. This makes parts of the machine turn. Some **sewing machines** and small **lathes** are operated by a treadle.

She worked the treadle and began to sew a seam.

trolley *noun*

A trolley is a wheeled **vehicle** which is pushed by hand. It is used to carry luggage at railway stations and airports or to carry goods from shops.

The supermarket trolley was full of the food they had bought.

tumble drier *noun*

A tumble drier is an **appliance** for drying wet washing. It contains a **heater** and an **electric motor**. The washing is placed in a drum which is turned, or rotated, by the motor. As it rotates, warm air flows through the contents of the drum and dries them.

Our clothes were soaked by the rain, so we put them in the tumble drier.

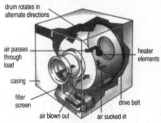

drum rotates in alternate directions

air passes through load

heater elements

casing

filter screen

drive belt

air blown out   air sucked in

tuner *noun*

A tuner is part of a **hi-fi** system. It selects the radio transmitter which has the programmes you want to hear. It has an **aerial** an **amplifier** and **loudspeakers**.

A tuner may be adjusted by turning a knob.

turbine *noun*

A turbine is a machine. Its **shaft** is connected to a set of curved blades separated by slits. A gas or liquid flows against the blades and through the slits which makes the blades turn, or rotate. This in turn spins the shaft of the turbine.

Turbines are used in power stations to produce electricity.

turbocharger *noun*

A turbocharger is a part of some **internal combustion engines**. It uses **exhaust gases** from the engine to drive a **turbine**. This runs another turbine which forces more air into the engine.

A turbocharger makes a car's engine very powerful.

turbofan *noun*
A turbofan is a kind of **jet engine**. It contains a **turbine** which is called a fan. This allows a blanket of air round the inside of the engine to be forced out through special jets. Turbofan engines are more efficient and quieter than other jet engines. They are sometimes called fanjets.
The airliner had turbofan engines and so it took off quietly.

turbojet *noun*
A turbojet is a kind of **jet engine**. It has a **compressor** which compresses the air entering the intake. This **compressed air** is mixed with fuel and set alight, or ignited. The force of hot gases being pushed out of the exhaust drives the engine forward.
The airliner was powered by four turbojets.

turnstile *noun*
A turnstile is a **device** which counts the number of people passing through a gate. Each person passing through moves a **lever** which operates a counter. Turnstiles are used at sports grounds and in some supermarkets.
There was a crowd waiting to go through the turnstiles at the football ground.

revolving barrier
ratchet

turntable *noun*
A turntable is a kind of machine. It has a motor which makes a flat surface turn round, or rotate. The turntable of a record player makes the record rotate.
Large turntables are used to turn railway engines round.

turning tool *noun*
A turning tool is a tool which is used to shape objects on a **lathe**. Turning tools include cutting, scraping and polishing tools. They are made of hardened steel.
He used turning tools to shape the leg of the chair with his lathe.

tweezers *plural noun*
Tweezers are small tools which are used for very accurate work with small objects. They have two jaws which are squeezed together to pick objects up.
Watchmakers use tweezers when they make or mend watches.

twin-rotor helicopter *noun*
A twin-rotor helicopter is an **aircraft**. It is a large **helicopter** with two sets of rotor blades mounted above the **fuselage**. Twin-rotor helicopters used by soldiers are sometimes called helicopter gunships.
There were many passengers on board the twin-rotor helicopter.

two-stroke engine *noun*
A two-stroke engine is an **internal combustion engine**. Each stroke moves a **piston** up or down inside a cylinder to make power. The fuel and air enter the cylinder through a slot in the cylinder wall. The exhaust gas leaves through another slot. There are only two moving parts in a two-stroke engine, the piston and the crank.
Small motor cycles often have two-stroke engines.

typesetting machines *noun*
Typesetting machines are machines which lay out type ready for printing. Some typesetting machines use molten metal which is poured into moulds. Modern typesetting machines are similar to word processors. They produce printed sheets called camera-ready copy. This is photographed and made into a printing plate.
At the newspaper office, the news was being set into type by typesetting machines.

typewriter *noun*
A typewriter is a machine which produces printed letters and numbers. It is operated by pressing keys on a **keyboard**. The type is on separate metal bars, on a daisy-wheel or on a round, metal ball which is called a golfball. A typewriter can be operated by hand or powered by an **electric motor**.
He typed the letter on his typewriter.

U

tyre *noun*
A tyre is the covering on the outside edge of a wheel. It can be made of solid rubber or it can be a **pneumatic** tyre. A tyre has a pattern on its surface which is called the tread. This helps it to grip the road.
I went to the cycle shop and bought two new tyres for my bicycle.

ultrasound scanner *noun*
An ultrasound scanner is a **device** used in hospitals. It allows doctors to look at parts inside the body. An ultrasound scanner sends **very high frequency** sound waves into the body and records the echoes. Ultrasound scanners work in a similar way to **sonar**. The results can be viewed on a television screen or print-out.
The doctor used an ultrasound scanner to study his patient's heart.

undercarriage ► landing gear

uranium *noun*
Uranium is a very heavy metal which is used in **nuclear reactors**. It makes the energy on which **nuclear power stations** run. Uranium also gives out dangerous radiation.
Uranium must be handled with great care because it can damage living tissues.

vacuum   *noun*
A vacuum is a space which contains no material of any kind. Liquids and gases try to fill a vacuum if they can. Vacuums are used in some **pumps**. A complete vacuum can only be found in outer space.
A vacuum flask or jug is a glass container surrounded by a vacuum.

vacuum cleaner   *noun*
A vacuum cleaner is an **appliance** which is used in the home. It contains a fan which makes a partial **vacuum** inside the body of the cleaner. Air from outside rushes in to fill the vacuum, and sucks dust and dirt in with it.
She used a vacuum cleaner to clean the carpets.

valve   *noun*
A valve is a **device** which controls the flow of a liquid or gas through an opening. It can be opened or shut. Some valves allow a liquid or gas to flow in only one direction.
The water engineer turned a stop valve in the street to stop the flow of water.

VCR ► **video cassette recorder**

VDU ► **visual display unit**

vehicle   *noun*
A vehicle is a machine for travelling over land. Cars, trucks, tractors and vans are all kinds of vehicle. They are powered by **internal combustion engines** which use either petrol or diesel fuel. Some vehicles have **electric motors**.
The path is meant for walkers only and no vehicles are allowed on it.

vending machine   *noun*
A vending machine is a machine which **automatically** supplies goods when money is put into a slot. Vending machines can stock sweets, hot or cold drinks, sandwiches and other goods.
He put some money in the vending machine and bought an orange drink.

vertical take-off and landing aircraft
noun
A vertical take-off and landing aircraft, or VTOL, is an **aeroplane** which can take off and land without using a runway. It can also use a very short runway. VTOLs have jet engines with jets that can be turned sideways or downwards to give power for turning or rising. Vertical take-off and landing aircraft are sometimes used on a type of **warship** called an aircraft carrier.
A jump jet is a vertical take-off and landing aircraft.

very high frequency   *adjective*
Very high frequency describes radio or
sound waves. Very high frequency radio
waves carry radio and television signals.
Very high frequency sound waves are used
in **sonar** and **ultrasound scanners**. The
abbreviation for very high frequency is VHF.
*The policemen talked to each other on their
very high frequency radios.*

vessel   *noun*
1. A vessel is another word for a **ship**, or
large boat that is designed to carry cargo or
passengers.
*There were 100 passengers on the vessel
when it left port.*
2. A vessel is a container. It may be made
of metal, glass or plastic. The vessel of a
steel converter holds liquid, or molten, metal.
*The vessel was tipped and molten steel
poured out into moulds.*

VHF ► **very high frequency**

vice   *noun*
A vice is a tool. It grips objects on which
work is being done. Its grip is made tighter
or looser by turning a **lever**. The lever is
attached to a shaft which has a thread like a
bolt.
*The carpenter put the piece of wood in a
vice so that it would not move around while
he was planing it.*

video camera ► **television camera**

video cassette recorder   *noun*
A video cassette recorder is a machine
which records and plays back moving
pictures and sound. A television camera
changes light and sound into **electric
signals**. These signals are transferred to
magnetic tape when it passes the **tape
heads** inside the recorder. When a recording
is played back, the tape heads receive
signals from the tape and pass them to a
screen and a **loudspeaker**.
*A video cassette recorder is useful for
recording television programmes to watch
later.*

viewdata   *noun*
Viewdata is a method of exchanging
information by **computer**. A number of
computers are connected together by
telephone lines and can then communicate
with each other. Information can be
channelled into hospitals, shops and other
businesses. Many travel agents use
viewdata.
*Viewdata can be used to shop for goods by
using a computer.*

viewfinder   *noun*
A viewfinder is part of a **camera**. It shows
photographers what will be seen in the
pictures that they take. Some kinds of
viewfinder contain a **lens** which is separate
from the lens through which the picture is
taken. In a **single lens reflex camera** the
same lens is used.
*She looked through the viewfinder and
asked her friends to move closer to each
other.*

vinyl   *noun*
Vinyl is a plastic material. It is used to make
many different objects. Vinyl can be used to
make cloth for covering furniture. It can also
be made into hard objects, such as bowls.
Vinyl is made at a factory from natural
substances, such as salt, natural gas and
petroleum.
The armchairs had a vinyl covering.

visual display unit *noun*
A visual display unit, or VDU for short, is a
part of a **computer**. It has a **screen** similar
to the screen of a television set. The screen
of a visual display unit shows **data** which is
typed on a **keyboard** and the work that the
computer has done.
He pressed a key and new data appeared
on the visual display unit.

VTOL ► **vertical take-off and landing
aircraft**

warhead *noun*
A warhead is a part of a bomb, **torpedo** or
missile. It contains an explosive which is set
on fire, or detonated, when the warhead
reaches the target. Modern explosives are
harmless until a detonator is attached.
Some submarines can fire missiles with
nuclear warheads.

warship ► page 152

washer *noun*
1. A washer is a small, flat **disc** of metal or
fibre with a hole in the centre. A **bolt** passes
through the hole and a nut is threaded onto
the bolt. The washer holds the nut and bolt
tightly together.
The nut worked loose because he had
forgotten to put a washer on the bolt.
2. A washer is a part of a **tap** or **valve**. It is
made of a soft material such as rubber
which can be squeezed. A washer stops a
liquid or gas leaking through a closed tap or
valve.
The plumber came to fit a new washer
because the bath tap was leaking.

washing machine *noun*
A washing machine is an **appliance** which
automatically does the washing. The
washing is placed in a drum with detergent.
The drum fills with water and turns, or
rotates. When the washing is clean, it is
rinsed and the water is pumped out. Some
washing machines contain a **spin drier** or a
tumble drier.
She collected the family's dirty clothes and
put them in the washing machine.

watch *noun*
A watch is a **device** for telling the time. Most watches are worn on the wrist. Some have a **clockwork motor** and others are driven by electricity from a tiny button **battery**.
He looked at his watch and saw that he was going to be late.

water closet ► lavatory

water-cooled *adjective*
Water-cooled describes a machine which has cold water flowing around it to stop it becoming too hot. A series of pipes carries the water around a water-cooled machine. A **fan** is often used to keep the water cold. Most **internal combustion engines** are water-cooled.
He filled the motor car's radiator with water to stop the water-cooled engine overheating.

water gauge *noun*
A water gauge describes a **device** for measuring the depth of water in a vessel, such as a tank.
He checked the level of water in the kettle by looking at the water gauge.

water turbine *noun*
A water turbine is a machine. It has a shaft which is driven by water flowing through the slits between the turbine blades. Water turbines are found in **hydroelectric power stations**.
Water from the fast-flowing river provided energy to make the water turbine work.

waterwheel *noun*
A waterwheel is a **wheel** which is made to turn by flowing water. Blades stand out from the hub of the waterwheel so that the water falls onto them.
Waterwheels can be used to drive pumps and other machines.

wave power ► tidal energy

weaving machine ► loom

web offset printing press *noun*
A web offset printing press is a machine which prints by **offset lithography**. It prints onto a reel of paper which is called a web. The printed web is then passed through a drier and into a folder which cuts and folds the paper. This produces folded sections that are bound together to make a book.
Most newspapers are printed on web offset printing presses.

weighbridge *noun*
A weighbridge is a **weighing machine**. It is used for weighing **vehicles** and their loads. The vehicle is driven on to a platform. The platform sinks with the vehicle and the amount it sinks is shown on a dial. This gives the weight of the vehicle.
The driver drove his truck on to the platform of the weighbridge.

weighing machine ► page 154

warship *noun*

A warship is a **ship** designed to take part in war. **Frigates**, destroyers, aircraft carriers and most **submarines** are kinds of warship. *There were several naval warships docked at the port.*

An aircraft carrier is the largest and most powerful warship. It has a flight deck with special equipment. This allows aircraft, such as fighter and bomber planes, to take off and land without a runway. Aircraft carriers also carry helicopters and other small kinds of plane.

A frigate is used mainly to defend other ships against enemy submarines. They carry anti-submarine weapons, such as torpedoes and nuclear depth charges.

A patrol craft is a small warship. It is used to guard rivers and coastal waters.

A destroyer carries guns, missiles and anti-submarine weapons. It defends other ships and also carries out search and rescue missions at sea.

weighing machine   *noun*

A weighing machine is a machine which measures the weight of objects.
Kitchen scales, spring balances and weighbridges are kinds of weighing machine.

A French mathematician called Roberval designed this weighing machine in 1669. Known as the Roberval enigma, it weighs objects accurately using two pans. The object to be weighed is placed in one pan and weights are placed in the other to balance the object. Simple kitchen scales are based on this design.

Bathroom scales are platform scales. They have a strong spring which is squeezed, or compressed, when a person stands on the platform. A system of other springs and levers works together to turn the dial to the correct weight.

These scales have a spring mechanism inside, which moves the hand on the dial when a weight is placed in the pan.

This simple design using two pans and weights was based on the Roberval enigma.

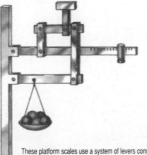

These platform scales use a system of levers connected together by vertical bars. The main lever has a scale marked on it and a sliding weight. An object is placed on the platform. The main lever moves up and the weight is slid along the scale until all the levers balance.

This spring balance is useful for weighing awkward objects, such as heavy suitcases. An object is hung on the hook which pulls down a very strong spring. This moves the marker on the scale to show the object's weight.

wheel *noun*

A wheel is a **disc** which turns, or rotates, round a **shaft** or **axle**. Bicycles, cars and trucks travel on wheels which are fitted with rubber tyres. **Gears** are wheels with cogs. *Most cars have four wheels, and most motor-cycles have two.*

The first wheels known to have been used on vehicles were made with three planks of wood joined by wooden struts. The Sumerians used such wheels about 5,000 years ago on their chariots.

Wheels were probably first used thousands of years ago for making pottery. Today, potters' wheels are sometimes turned by electric motors.

A modern bicycle wheel is made of aluminium, which is strong but very lightweight. Thin metal spokes support the outer rim.

Waterwheels are still used in some countries to drive simple machines.

Some road vehicles have huge wheels to carry them over rough ground.

Gear wheels, such as this bevel gear, are used in many machines to pass, or transmit, energy from one part to another.

welding *noun*
Welding is a method of joining pieces of metal. The usual method of welding is to melt the edges of the metal so that they join together, or fuse, without a break.
The different parts of a car body are joined by welding.

welding torch

oxygen

oxy-acetylene

welding torch *noun*
A welding torch is a tool. It produces a very hot flame which is used to **weld** pieces of metal together. The flame comes from burning gases, which are usually oxygen and acetylene.
The mechanic used a welding torch to mend the broken metal part.

wheel ► page 156

wheelbarrow *noun*
A wheelbarrow is a **simple machine** used by builders and gardeners. It is a kind of **lever**. A wheelbarrow allows a person to do more work than could be done by lifting and carrying.
The builder used a wheelbarrow to carry the concrete for the path.

whisk *noun*
A whisk is a **device** used in cooking. It is used to mix the whites and yolks of eggs and for other purposes. A whisk can be operated by hand or by an **electric motor**.
She used a whisk to beat the eggs to make an omelette.

winch *noun*
A winch is a **simple machine** for lifting objects. It is operated by turning a **wheel** with a handle. A rope is wound round the wheel and hooked onto the object being lifted.
They hauled the boat up the slipway with a winch.

wind power *noun*
Wind power describes the use of the wind to **generate electricity** or operate **machines**. The wind can spin a **turbine** or a **propeller**. In this way, wind energy is changed to mechanical or electrical energy.
Scientists hope that one day more electricity will be generated by wind power.

wind tunnel *noun*
A wind tunnel is a **device** for testing how **aircraft** will behave at different air speeds. Winds of different strengths are made by a **fan** driven by an **electric motor**. Engineers sometimes test **models**, or even full-size aircraft, in wind tunnels.
The wind tunnel test showed that the aircraft would give a bumpy flight in high winds.

wind turbine *noun*
A wind turbine is a machine which **generates electricity** by using **wind power**. The wind blows through the blades of a small **turbine** which is connected to a **generator**. Electricity is made when the turbine blades rotate. Most wind turbines are mounted on a swivel on top of a tower. This means that they can be turned to face the wind when it changes direction.
Wind turbines work well if they are built in places where there are strong winds.

windmill *noun*
A windmill is a machine which makes use of **wind power**. It has blades or sails which are driven round by the wind. Many years ago, windmills were used to grind wheat into flour.
The sails of the windmill drove a shaft which turned and made the grindstone move.

windscreen wiper   *noun*
A windscreen wiper is a **device** which clears
rain and dirt from the windscreen of a
vehicle. It has one or more blades driven by
an **electric motor**.
*It was raining hard, so the driver switched on
the windscreen wipers.*

wireless ► **radio**

word processor   *noun*
A word processor is a special kind of
computer. It has a keyboard, a central
processing unit, a visual display unit and a
printer. As words are typed, they appear on
the screen. When typing is finished, the
words are printed out.
*It is easy to correct mistakes on a word
processor.*

worm gear   *noun*
A worm gear is a part of some machines.
Unlike other **gears**, a worm gear has a
continuous thread, like a **screw**. A gear
wheel turns a second gear wheel called a
worm, which is set at right angles.
*Worm gears change the direction of a drive
by 90 degrees.*

X-ray   *noun*
An X-ray is a **very high frequency**
electromagnetic wave. X-ray machines can
show the insides of bodies. Doctors use
X-rays to inspect patients' lungs and to
check for broken bones.
*After his fall, he went to the hospital for an
X-ray to check that no bones were broken.*

zoom lens   *noun*

A zoom lens is a **device** used in a **camera**.
It is made up of a number of **lenses**. A zoom
lens makes it appear that the camera is
moving quickly towards an object.
*Zoom lenses are used with still, television
and movie cameras.*